Wild Child

Wrong Place, Right Time

Tracy Miller

Wild Child
Copyright © 2021 by Tracy Miller
All Rights Reserved

All rights reserved. No part of this publication may be reproduced, distributed, or transmitted in any form or by any means, including photocopying, recording, or other electronic or mechanical methods, without the prior written permission of the AUTHOR, except in the case of brief quotations embodied in critical reviews and certain other noncommercial uses permitted by copyright law. This book is intended for educational purposes only.

Publisher: Absolute Author Publishing House
Publishing Editor: Dr. Melissa Caudle
Editor: David Dubos
Junior Editor: Paul S. Dupre
Cover Design: Teresa Cacho

Paperback ISBN: 978-1-64953-284-8
eBook ISBN: 978-1-64953-285-5

Dedication

I'd like to dedicate this book to my mother Geraldine Eddleston Miller for her undying love and support for me during all of my trials and tribulations. And, most importantly for not killing me as an infant. Thank you also for your encouraging words, "It's alright son, you'll do better next time."

Special Thanks

I would like to thank Dr. Mel Caudle for all of her help and guidance in the publishing of this, my first book.

I want to thank David Dubos for taking the time to do a superb job, in editing *Wild Child*.

I'd like to thank Teresa Cacho for using her incredible talent as an artist in creating the cover art for my book.

I also want to thank Tanner Miller, Cheryl Zlaket, Heather Waite, Richard Gonzales, and Bruce Mayes for their invaluable help in proof reading *Wild Child* and their wonderful suggestions on sculpting this memoir.

TABLE OF CONTENTS

Chapter 1...1

Chapter 2...4

Chapter 3...10

Chapter 4...13

Chapter 5...15

Chapter 6...24

Chapter 7...27

Chapter 8...32

Chapter 9...37

Chapter 10...40

Chapter 11...46

Chapter 12...48

Chapter 13...50

Chapter 14...54

Chapter 15...56

Chapter 16...60

Chapter 17...62

Chapter 18...64

Chapter 19...66

Chapter 20...69

Chapter 21...73

Chapter 22...78

Chapter 23...82

Chapter 24...85

Chapter 25...89

Chapter 26	91
Chapter 27	93
Chapter 28	95
Chapter 29	97
Chapter 30	104
Chapter 31	110
Chapter 32	113
Chapter 33	116
Chapter 34	120
Chapter 35	124
Chapter 36	129
Chapter 37	130
Chapter 38	131
Chapter 39	135
Chapter 40	139
Chapter 41	142
Chapter 42	148
Chapter 43	155
Chapter 44	159
Chapter 45	162
Chapter 46	165
Chapter 47	169
Chapter 48	174
Chapter 49	180
Chapter 50	184
Chapter 51	186

Chapter 52 188
Chapter 53 190
Chapter 54 194
Chapter 55 196
Chapter 56 198

Chapter 1

A Life-Changing Decision

I was twenty-one and cruising around my hometown of Orange, California, in my multi-colored '61 VW Baja Bug on a sunny day in the summer of 1977 with my friend Diz, when I decided to stop by my friend Tim Grieves' house. It was a fateful detour.

We knocked and walked in and found a little gathering of Tim, Bruce Mayes, Jim Barnes, and Clinton Skaggs. We all went to school together. They were discussing a European trip they were going to take later in the year. As I listened, I began to get excited by the concept of hitting the road again. I had taken little trips, off and on, for several years. When I was seventeen and just days out of high school, I hitchhiked to Alaska and back with Tim's older brother, Larry (or Sparky, as he was known to his

After listening for a while, I thought my friends' plans sounded cool, and I wanted to hit the road again, but I didn't know if I wanted to travel with a gang of people on a trip like this one. Traveling in bunches can be difficult. Two is a good number, but one is even better.

I mean, who'd be in charge of our itinerary? What about food and lodging? What if one or more of us wanted to take a side trip to a more interesting destination? With a lot of people, you have to go with the crowd. And when you travel in groups, you have your own environment, so to speak, you bring with you all from your homeland.

You don't reach out as much as you do when you're by yourself. You're much more apt to experience the local culture and people of a country when you're by yourself than you do when you're with a bunch of friends from home. It's almost as if you have no choice but to immerse yourself in your surroundings when you're alone.

I just figured it wasn't for me. So, I thought I'd just hang out with my buds for a while, drink some beers and smoke some pot. But the more I listened, the more intrigued I got. I thought, why not travel with a group, especially this group, my good friends. I had been itching to do something like this for a while, and this would be the perfect fit. I could hit the road with my pals and then branch off on my own.

After a couple of hours of getting slowly drunk and stoned, I finally gave in and asked if it would be alright if I went with them. They were unanimous in their answer. Hell, yes!

Together, we planned out the trip and departure. Bruce, an experienced overseas traveler, had made previous trips to Europe and the Middle East and had some great ideas about where to go and what to do. Bruce was kind of our de facto leader for this trip.

He was a former football player, a tall, good-looking kid who the girls seemed to like. We'd known each other since junior high and were always good friends. He liked to party a good deal and liked the ladies, and that was just fine by me.

Tim was more like me, a free-spirited guy into ditching school and body surfing. Eventually, Tim would ditch his family, a large Catholic unit of ten kids, mostly boys. Tim's parents decided California was a little too wild a place to raise their brood, so they moved to the Mid-West, but Tim stayed behind. He was always an independent-minded guy, again like me.

Jim was another football player from my school, but unlike Bruce, he was more of a mauler, a tree-trunk for a torso but an easy-going guy. Jim would only be with us on the trip for a month, as he had a serious relationship and a good job. So, he'd be heading back home after a short while.

WILD CHILD

Clinton, like Bruce and Jim, was athletic, a star running back. We had been friends since 10th grade when we met in agriculture class with Mr. Tobler. He was just someone I hit it off with right away, and it was 'Love at First Bite,' so to speak. The only problem with him was that he drank the wrong brand of beer.

Even though I wasn't much of a jock, I still fit in with this cast of characters. While I did like smoking pot, I wasn't a lazy stoner. I had plans, big plans, for my future. I wanted to be an actor. This was a dream of mine since I got involved in Community Theatre at the age of eight. It was my life's dream, and my mantra was embodied by T.S. Elliott's famous statement, "Dream your dreams, young man, but have the courage to make them come true."

I had already begun my journey into being a professional actor by sitting in classes in Los Angeles, searching for a teacher I wanted to study with, someone who would hopefully guide me to my inner voice as an artist. But that costs money; lots of money. And I spent a lot of it pursuing that voice. I still hadn't found it (yet), but after looking over the travel plans in front of me, I decided my Hollywood hopes would have to be put on hold, as the wanderlust in me was making a much louder noise.

After a few more beers and a few more tokes, the plan for our epic trip was completed. It sounded like fun, almost a fantasy, and I didn't realize it then, but this was the beginning of a journey that would ultimately change my life. Now all I needed was money.

Chapter 2

In The Beginning

I come from a large family: Dad, Mom, and four boys, no girls. Dad was a career military man, having served twenty-eight years in the Marine Corps, mainly as a Gunnery Sergeant. He was a navigator for C-130 cargo planes and the perfect age to hit the Marine Trifecta as a veteran of World War II, the Korean War, and the Vietnam War.

I was the middle child, third in line, and like a typical middle child, I was the black sheep of the family. I was my Father's main nemesis growing up, his golden bad boy, and got much of his unwanted attention.

I come from the time of corporal punishment, which is essentially your parents (and occasional teachers) beat the crap out of you if you misbehaved. My Dad never held back. He wasn't shy about handing out punishment.

He was also a barracks commander, and, as such, you didn't talk back to the Gunny. You also didn't say things like "No" or "Fuck you" to the Gunny, either. But I did, and he'd have a serious go at me regularly, often going overboard with physical discipline.

My oldest brother Bob once told me he and my brothers used to pray that I wouldn't say anything to Dad after an ass-whooping. But as he walked away, I just couldn't help myself. I felt he was wrong, and I called him out on it. That only pissed him off more, which meant another round of ass-kicking was coming my way.

My Mother, Geraldine, or Gerry to her friends, was a tall woman, about 5'8", and a strong but loving woman of English, Irish, and French descent. My Father and she met while working in a coffee shop at the pier in Newport Beach. At the time, my Mom was living on her father's (my grandfather's) boat in Balboa Harbor. She was all of eighteen, and my father was then twenty-five and already in the Marine Corps.

Mom was happiest and at her best when she was with her extended family. That was what she lived for, but she was also someone you didn't want to irritate. When I was young, she didn't hesitate to let me have it when I was out of line, which was most of the time. Often, she'd have a go at me for whatever I did, and when Dad got home, he would have his turn. This was not out of the ordinary for the time.

And if I'm honest with myself, I deserved my punishment. I made life hell for my parents. It started very early, and eight was a big year for me. I began smoking cigarettes, got drunk for the first time, was arrested for breaking and entering, started hanging out in pool halls, and ran away from home for the first time.

I was also one of the original Ritalin kids. But I didn't enjoy taking it, so I gave them to my friends to take, as I was already taking my preferred drugs by the age of twelve.

As I got older, my troubles with the law and at school continued. I was always getting booted out of school and arrested. Finally, my parents couldn't take it anymore. I moved out of their house for the first time during the summer between 11th and 12th grade. I was sixteen years old, and I started dealing pot, drinking more, and using heavier drugs. In short, I was one of those lost kids.

Compared to me, my brothers were practically angels, pure as snow. My oldest brother, Bob, was the total opposite of me. Physically, we were both tall, but that's where all similarities ended. Bob never got in trouble and never did drugs, and that's saying a lot for his character, given that the eras of the '60s and '70s were the epitome of the drug culture.

Bob did, however, join a Christian cult in 1970. At that time, cults were big, especially in California. Though they are often associated with violence (such as the Manson family), others were more benign, such as the one that Bob joined. Bob lived with the cult for seventeen years. During that time, he met and married his first wife, Sue, and they had two beautiful sons together, Kody and Bobby Lee. After he left the cult, we became closer and shared our common love for creativity and the arts. In many ways, Bob was a dreamer, like me, having written many short stories and a couple of novels. We supported each other in pursuing our dreams.

Unfortunately, Bob passed away at forty-nine from a very aggressive case of liver cancer. It's true that only the good die young.

Carey, my other old brother, is two years my senior and, outside of my father, my main nemesis growing up. He didn't get the tall gene like my other siblings and me, standing only about 5'8', but he was highly intelligent and had a sharp wit that could cut to the bone. We fought a lot as kids, verbally and physically, but Carey was always there to protect me whenever I got into a fight with another kid at school or on the playground. He, too, was a jock and didn't fool around with dope. Later on, he followed Bob into the cult in 1971. And like Bob, he met and married his wife, Carol, there. And following Bob's lead, he and I became close once he left the cult as an adult.

After me, there is my brother Rick, two years my junior. Of all my brothers, he and I were the closest while growing up. We got along very well as kids and played together a lot. It was two camps: Bob and Carey, and Rick and me. Unlike me, Rick was a cheerful kid and always had this big smile on his face. Like my brothers, Rick was a jock and never got involved with drugs or drinking. I've always felt I let him down when we were teenagers, as I was into heavy drugs and wasn't there for him, and possibly, as a result, he, too, ended up in the cult in 1975, following our older brothers' path. True, it was better that Rick didn't follow my wayward path, but I strongly feel that the cult stole their lives as young men. After he left the cult, he married his first wife, Maria, and had a beautiful, spunky daughter, Jessi. He is now married to his second wife, Joy, and they have a wonderful life together.

And then there was James, who came into our lives in 1968 while Dad served in Vietnam. I was thirteen and into psychedelics, pot, and more. I wasn't ready to be a Dad, but we were all forced into becoming surrogate fathers to our baby brother because of circumstances. After he was born, my Mother had to go right back to work so there would be a steady income flowing into the house.

James would eventually follow my brothers into the same cult while he was still in high school. He's now married to an exceptional woman, Lisa, and they have a beautiful daughter, Emerson.

Compared to me, my brothers were angels. Before I hit the international road for my whirlwind trip with my friends, I got into a ton of trouble. Trouble at home, in school, and with the police. Most of the time, my misdeed were just misdemeanors. That is until I turned eighteen and was old enough to go to real jail.

As a minor, I always was released to my parents. Nothing too bad, certainly nothing violent, so I avoided juvenile jail. I was just a wayward and very mischievous kid. The things I wasn't supposed to do just seemed much more interesting, intoxicating, and fascinating to me, like a bee drawn to honey. I didn't have a black soul or anything evil like that; just a kid headed down the wrong path. I had a high IQ and could have easily excelled in school, but it didn't interest me. The kids that got good grades didn't interest me either, and it would have taken more work than I was willing to put out in school to get A's and B's, so instead, I got D's and F's. And as a hyperactive kid, I couldn't sit still long enough to study, so I was always in trouble early on, and over the years, it just escalated from there. I guess I was that typical "Rebel Without a Cause," or as Tom Petty once sang, a "Rebel Without a Clue."

My career as a criminal reached its apex or nadir (depending on your perspective) when I hit nineteen. That year, I hit the trouble trifecta. I was arrested for the cultivation of marijuana (200 plants), a kilo of pot, window pane LSD, and a powder cut used for cocaine, all for sale. I was looking at thirty-five years in prison, but my attorney got me off on the technicalities of the search and seizure laws.

Many years later, my older brother Carey told me he and my brothers and their friends constantly prayed for me. He believed angels must be looking after me because, obviously, I wasn't thinking or looking after myself. Instead, I was on autopilot, just living by my gut instincts and feelings.

My first hero, or real father figure, was my grandfather on my mother's side, Robert Eddleston. He was an intelligent, successful businessman and very kind to my brothers and me. He had a 55' boat in Balboa Harbor, and my first visual memories of life are on that boat with Bob, Carey, and our cousin Chris going through the break waters at the mouth of the bay and further out into the Pacific Ocean while sitting on the bow of the boat. I wrote Grandpa Robert letters as a young child, and in my travels, we wrote to each other. He was the first person to suggest that I was a storyteller and should become a writer. He lived ninety-eight years and had a great life.

I had no desire to continue my formal education by going to college. I don't think my parents had any actual plans for me. They were more worried about keeping me alive into adulthood. When I told them of my plan and desire to be an actor, they probably heaved a sigh of relief.

The acting bug came about for several reasons, but it all boiled down to this: I couldn't relate to my father's life. It wasn't for me. I wanted more out of my life, and because of the violent clashes we had early on, I had no relationship or communication with him as a child and as a young man.

Fortunately, years later, I forgave my father, and he did the same for me. When I was in my mid-thirties, we were at an impasse, sort of a no-fault blame game. This wasn't surprising to me. I knew there was no way he would ever admit any wrongdoing on his part; maybe it was the Marine in him, full of pride, piss, and vinegar. But, from his perspective, he was right to dole out discipline to his unruly child.

From my point of view, however, I was no different from any other rebellious kid who looked upon their Father as square, out-of-touch, or someone who didn't understand me or my generation. There was plenty of blame to go around on both sides, but at least I could reconcile with my dad years later before he passed. Most kids can't say that and instead allowed a past feud, a chip on their shoulder, or bitterness and resentment to impede moving on with their life.

It was a wonderful relationship for me and my pop and my three children, Trevor, Caitlin, and Tanner. He was able to be the father he always wanted to be with his kids but wasn't capable of, but he was with my kids. And it was a beautiful thing to see.

Of course, hindsight is 20/20, and I didn't have that benefit at the time. All I knew was that I wanted to get out on my own, be my own man, explore the world, make that my own private college education. I figured the lessons I learned would be worth a helluva lot more than a piece of paper sitting in a cheap frame.

Chapter 3

Preparing

My decision was set, as was the rough date of departure: late November or early December. I left Tim's house feeling very excited and optimistic about my future. I went to my parents' house and told them all about my grand plans. I had moved back into their home a few months before to save on rent, so I figured this would be a great opportunity for me to bank some good money for the trip. Or so I hoped.

I worked on the docks in Orange as a Teamster, loading and unloading trucks for local trucking companies. I'd work anywhere from four to eight hours at one location and then hurry over to another and pick up another four to eight hours. I was in the union and was well paid. With the trip less than six months away, I would put in as many hours as I could handle and make as much money as I could.

I went shopping for new camping gear. I found a great backpack with an interior frame of strong metal that zipped open in the front. This style was much better than one that loaded from the top since you could pack your clothes away neatly and get to them without having to pull everything out to get to something at the bottom of your pack. And I bought a high-end goose-down sleeping bag in case I had to sleep outside during the harsh European winters.

During my trek to Alaska with Sparky, I used an old canvas backpack with an exterior aluminum frame that took in water. No sooner had I arrived in Alaska, and it broke on me. I also made a terrible decision in using a cotton sleeping bag that took in all the rain in

Alaska, and it rains a lot up in Ketchikan. I wasn't making those mistakes again, as I had no idea how long I would be gone.

I worked hard and often for five months and cut down on going to bars during the week to save even more money. However, I still went out on weekends; after all, I wasn't preparing to be a monk.

Between working and living frugally, I managed to save close to $4,000 by mid-November. Not a lot of money in today's dollars, but this was 1977, so it would last for a while. Besides, other than drinking, I traveled cheaply.

One night, I was on the dock at CME, a local company where I worked. The night manager walked over to me and said to come with him. There was some theft going on at the docks during my shift, and it was my turn to be questioned.

The man doing the interrogating was a real hard ass. He asked if I had taken anything.

"I don't do that," was my reply.

Then he asked if I knew who was stealing.

"I don't do that," was my repeated response.

"Don't do what?" he asked sternly.

I knew who the thief was, but I told him I didn't rat people out since I didn't like his braggadocios attitude. It wasn't my way, and if you need to fire me for that, so be it. Then I got up and went back to work.

When I came in the next night, the night manager called me into his office again. I figured this was it, and I was being fired. Instead, he offered me a job in sales or management when I returned from my trip in three months. I told him 'thank you' and that I'd definitely think about it. Little did I know I wouldn't be back in three months.

I only had a couple of weeks left before my departure. I worked as hard as I could, squeezing out every cent I could earn during my remaining time stateside. I then went around to say my goodbyes to family and friends. Perhaps deep down, I started to feel and believe that I wouldn't be back for a long time.

My girlfriend Theresa and I talked about the possibility of a longer trip than expected, but I was still talking about returning in a few months. Truth be told, I just didn't know at that point how long I'd be gone. On the one hand, I had a complete life in Orange: a girlfriend, a decent, well-paying job, good friends, and, of course, my family.

On the other hand, I was facing the possibility of discovering the world with my good friends and having a blast while doing so. There were so many opportunities opening up in front of me; there was an air of mystery about it all. Where would I end up traveling? How long would I be staying there? Would I meet someone else along the way? In a way, I was reverting to my bad boy days as a kid. Plunging headfirst into the unknown was thrilling, exciting, and intoxicating to me. Irresponsible? Maybe. Dangerous? Perhaps. But I needed a change of scenery. It was time to take my first proper steps into adulthood.

In two weeks, I'd board a plane for a foreign country for the first time besides Mexico. There was no turning back. And honestly, I couldn't wait.

Chapter 4

The Departure

December 5, 1977, was our departure date for London, our first stop on our international trek. A five-day round-trip ticket on Sir Freddy Laker's Airline would set me back a total of $99. Of course, we were planning to be on the road for a lot more than just five days, but the only way we could grab such a cheap ticket was to get a round-trip one instead of just one-way. I know that's hard to believe, but this was the most frugal way to travel back then, and Freddy Laker's was the most economical airline.

The night before our journey, we had a huge party at Clinton's house in Pico Rivera, a suburb of Los Angeles that was out in the boonies. So many friends were there that night, wishing us a fond farewell. It was a lot of fun, as those types of parties were back in the '70s. The party went on all night with drinking, talking, and doing way too much coke. I left about 5 a.m.., barely getting a couple of hours of sleep.

When I left home for the airport that morning, I had quite the hangover. Theresa and her friend Kristy drove me to the airport. My parents and kid brother, James, came to see me off, too.

By the time we pulled up to the airport, my friends were already waiting for the plane. My family hung around for an hour and then left. My father's parting words to me were along the lines of 'Have fun, but be safe, son.' He knew me all too well.

Once we were outside the building, Tim pulled out some pot brownies he had made and offered me one. Oddly, this was something

I never did, but in my current state, I thought,…well, I wasn't thinking, so I ate a big one. There was a delay in boarding the plane, so I figured why not.

I said goodbye to Theresa. We hugged and kissed, and I told her I'd write her from the road.

Except just as I was climbing the stairs to the plane, the brownies hit me like a ton of bricks. As I got to the top of the stairs, I turned to wave goodbye to Theresa and stumbled backward onto the plane.

I found my seat and my traveling companions: Bruce, Tim, and Jim, all of whom were already seated. Clinton and his girlfriend Carol were sitting by themselves a few rows behind us. Clinton had brought Carol along on our trip, as he was very much in love. In due time, she would become his wife.

I sat down, looked at them, and then turned around and vomited all over the floor and passed out.

Hours later, I woke up and realized the plane had landed in Maine for refueling. I looked around and saw a little boy a few seats up from me. He tapped his Mother on the shoulder and said, *"Mommy, look! There's that Man!"* What the hell? I've been called worse.

I got up and walked to the back of the plane because the door was open, and I wanted some fresh air. It was snowing and freezing outside, but it was just what I needed, as it helped to clear my head and wake me up. I made my way back to my seat and asked my friends if dinner had been served. I was starving. They informed me that dinner had come and gone, and yes, they were hungry as well. So hungry that they had eaten my dinner, too.

It was going to be a long flight.

Chapter 5

London and the Continent

It was a long flight, but by the time we landed at Heathrow Airport in London, I felt fine and ready for my new adventure.

Bruce led us to the Tube, London's version of a subway. We took it to the center of London and walked around for a while, searching for a cheap hotel. We found one in the Camden Town neighborhood of London and set about playing tourist, roaming around, seeing the sights.

In 1977, punk was king, and this was London, the epicenter of the punk movement. London has always had a reputation as a very fashionable city, for me starting with the mods and rockers fashion of the early '60s that segued to the "Swinging '60s" that erupted with gaudy, colorful clothes, shoes, and bling. And now, it was punk's turn, and trust me; punk fashion was on full display. It was quite a sight to see the fully dressed punk rockers all over the streets, shops, and parks… they were everywhere and impossible to avoid.

For me, though, the famous (and some infamous) pubs held sway, with their marvelous, old, and earthy atmosphere, just dripping with history. The only problem is that most of them only serve warm draft beer, not my forte or taste. It was my first sticker shock as an American, but hey, you either adapt or perish! So warm beer it was.

One night, we ventured into a pub with a pool table. Just my luck as I grew up in pool halls back home and played on bar league pool teams (and I still do to this day).

I patiently waited until it was my turn on the table. I had to adjust to the British rules, but I ruled the table for quite a while. It seemed to piss off the locals because who did this "focking yank" think he was!

I could feel the temperature in the room change, and for a moment, I thought we were going to get into a brawl. Now, Bruce and Jim were big guys, former football players. Tim was good-sized as well as I am. It would be a fair fight, except the Brits outnumbered us at least 4 to 1.

I quickly came to my senses and decided to tank the next game so that we could get out of there with nary a scratch, much less a broken nose, hand, or arm. Having lost the last game, I thanked our hosts, and we made a quick exit.

After spending several days in London, we headed for the southern coast to catch a ferry to Belgium. I was sitting on the ferry's bow eating a small salad I had bought at an English grocery store. London is a great city filled with grand architecture, the West End, the Royal Family, and, of course, lots of amazing pubs, but in the culinary department, English food leaves a lot to be desired. That's why grocery store food became our go-to dining experience because it was not only economical but easy on the taste buds as well.

In the middle of my meal, a young woman walked up and muttered something in a foreign language that sounded French. I did not know what she said, but Carol told me she said, *"Good appetite,"* aka *"Bon appétit."* She turned out to be Belgian, and so we talked for a while in broken English; then she gave me her phone number and said to call her when I was in Lint, near Antwerp, her hometown.

Clinton and Carol split from us soon after we arrived on the continent. After all, they were a young couple in love, and we were four wild men, dead set on drinking and partying our way through Europe, not an ideal mix for them, which from my groups' perspective was understandable.

While in London, we purchased Euro Rail passes that allow you to travel by train all over Europe for three months on a onetime ticket at a very reduced price.

One of our first stops was Luxembourg, and the most memorable thing I can recall was that it was the dead of winter and freezing cold. When I went to take a shower in a room outside the ancient hotel we were staying at; I realized they only had cold water. I was torn between my desire to get clean and my desire to avoid hypothermia. I think I set a world record for a shower that day.

I told my traveling group that I would take off for a few days to see the Belgium girl I had met on the ferry from England. Bruce and I set up a meeting place so we could hook up later in Antwerp, Belgium.

I hopped the train to her town, Lint, without calling her. That, in retrospect, was probably not a great idea. But I enjoyed traveling by instinct and enjoyed my time on the train, meeting lots of wonderful folks, and overall having a wonderful time.

I met an older Belgian gentleman who was headed to visit his grandchildren.

He asked where I was from and when he found out I was American, he told me he always had a desire to visit America. He had been a part of the Belgian underground forces during World War II and told me some fascinating stories of the time.

I also met two young guys around my age who were Belgians and headed to Amsterdam for a short vacation. They recommended a few places to go to while there. We ended up sharing a bottle of wine. One of them played the guitar, and once he started playing, we drew more young people and ended up with a little party eating bread, cheese and drinking more wine. I had to get off of the train, so we exchanged addresses. I told them to look me up if they were ever in California; I had a habit of doing this whenever I met friendly travelers.

I arrived in Lint mid-day and went immediately to the nearest phone booth to call my Belgian friend. Her mother answered the phone. I asked to speak to her daughter; she refused. Oh boy. My first taste of anti-American prejudice… or maybe it was just a wise mama acting as a buffer to protect her young daughter's reputation. I wasn't angry because I wouldn't allow my daughter to hook up with some strange foreigner if I have to be honest with myself. She knew what my endgame was. No matter. I had a great time meeting some wonderful people on the train. I rode the rails for a day, then head to Rotterdam to meet up with Bruce.

I regrouped with my mates. They were in their bathing suits in a Laundromat catching up on their washing. I followed suit and got into my swimmers in the middle of the European winter. It was nice finally to have clean clothes since that doesn't happen regularly when you're on the road.

We headed for Amsterdam the next day. Often referred to as the "Forbidden City," Amsterdam has the reputation as the Vice Capital of Europe, at least back then. They openly sold pot and hash in bars and clubs, and prostitution was 100% legal (and still is). There are cobblestoned streets with large windows, where beautiful ladies of the evening sit on chairs, all dolled up, ready-made for the lucrative business of sex.

We found a bar and hostel in the old part of the city that had a Southern vibe. It was named "The Last Watering Hole." It had a saddle and longhorns above the bar, with rebel flags draped from them. They played southern rock, especially The Allman Brothers and Charlie Daniels Band. It was a slice of Americana right in the middle of the Netherlands. So, naturally, for the homesick lads that we were, we hung out one night and got smashed.

The hostel was upstairs from the bar and had several bunk beds in the rooms. Since it was the off-season, we had a room to ourselves. We were sitting in the room smoking pot, relaxing when in walked Clinton and Carol. They had just arrived in Amsterdam and just happened to pick the same bar and hostel where we were staying.

All of us headed out that night to the downstairs bar. Between all the beer, booze, and pot, we were pretty wasted when we got back to the hostel. We stumbled upstairs and hit the sack.

Tim and I were sharing a bunk bed with me on top. Tim got sick that night and threw up in the trash can right next to his bed. Later, I heard a shuffling in the trash can and looked down in the middle of the night and saw some fairly large rats eating Tim's vomit. I banged on the locker next to the bed, and the rats ceased their disgusting meal. But moments later, they started again. I banged on the locker again, and they stopped again.

This continued throughout the night. I was having fun playing with the rats, but in my drunken state, I didn't think about the fact that they were right next to Tim's spinning head. Then I heard, *"Miller, Miller, Miller,"* coming from Tim in the bottom bunk. I stopped for a moment, banged hard one last time on the locker, and watched the rats jump out and escape.

Clinton and Carol left a few days later for points unknown. They were only going to be here for a short time, and they had an itinerary to follow.

We took off for Germany a couple of days later. I wasn't missing hitchhiking at the time because it was so cold and snowed often. Jim was only going to be with us for one month, and then he was heading back home, so we wanted to cover as many bases as possible while he was still with us. After his departure, Bruce, Tim, and I were planning on heading over to Greece and possibly Israel.

We stopped in Frankfurt and a few other large cities, but our primary destination was Munich and the Hofbräuhaus for some more drinking and fun. The Hofbräuhaus is a very large and cavernous beer hall in Munich and is famous the world over. They have huge wooden kegs of beer and play heavy German music all night long.

They also have large, tough, red-haired women serving you. You see them carrying several large glass mugs full of beer at a time. But you don't want to mess with them. They take care of most of the problems themselves, and the bouncers usually only show up when a fight breaks out.

We spent five nights in a row there having a great time. On our first night there, I wore a t-shirt that said, "Surfside, Newport Beach, California" on the back. We were drinking beer, minding our own business, when I heard this oddly accented man shout out, "Aussie surfers are the best surfers in the world."

We looked over, and four large guys were standing there staring at us. I thought and felt a fight brewing. We had a bit of a stand-off. Then they started smiling. They walked over to our table, introducing themselves. They were all from Australia and were both surfers and rugby players.

We spent the next few nights with them consuming massive amounts of beer and singing Aussie drinking songs. We really hit it off. On their last night there, we all exchanged contact information with the plans of visiting each other down the road.

One night there, I nearly got into a fight with a couple of American guys when out of nowhere, my red-headed bar maid came charging in, pushing the guys away from me. She was my protector from thereon out, always smiling at me. I think she took a liking to me.

We left the next day for Italy. The view was beautiful as we traveled through the European countryside. We would get food and beer in stores before boarding because it was too expensive to buy it on the train.

Our first stop in Italy was Venice, and it was all it was cracked up to be. The houses on the water, the bridges crossing the channels, the grand palaces, and the buildings were beautiful.

We found a small hotel in an alleyway off the canals. Then we headed out to see Saint Mark's Basilica in Piazza San Marco. It, too, lived up to its reputation, a stunningly beautiful place. We spent a couple of days touring around the city, then hopped the train to Florence. It was now December 30, and the plan was to spend New Year's Eve in Florence.

En route, we met a group of young Italian women about our age and had a lot of fun trying to talk to them. They spoke little English, and we certainly didn't speak Italian. What they knew in English were James Taylor songs and "Old McDonald Had a Farm."

We arrived at our destination, and much to our delight, the girls exited the train, too. It turned out they were also planning to spend New Year's in Florence, too. I hit it off with one of the women, and I was hoping I'd see her around town.

We found a pension on a nice street. The woman who owned the place was very strict and told us no alcohol or women in the room, and she meant it. I didn't think this was the pension for us, as we were here to party, which meant booze and women; all except Jim, who was in a relationship back home.

We went out that night and, as usual, drank and partied all night until they threw us out at closing time. We arrived back at the pension late and loud. The owner opened the door and wasn't too happy with our appearance and condition. She threw us out the next morning... early.

We went down the street trying to find a new pension, but it seemed she had called every pension on the street to tell them about us. Needless to say, we were getting a lot of verbal 'No Vacancies.'

We finally found one that would take us in. The owner was a friendly woman but told us she heard we were trouble. She said alcohol was fine, but not women. We told her we were good boys and promised her we'd behave. She laughed and said, 'Okay.'

That night, we went to a large disco that we had seen flyers for around town. The place was right out of Saturday Night Fever, and the locals were all dressed like John Travolta. And there we were in Levi's and t-shirts and bearded to boot. We looked more like hippies than disco dancers. We couldn't be accused of false advertising; what you saw with us is what you got with us.

Our Italian girls were there, looking marvelous in their disco garb. The girl I liked walked up to me, wanting to dance. She told me her name was Aurora, and she was from a small town in Sardinia. She was of average height, with short brown hair and a beautiful body and face, just like you'd imagine from the country that spawned Sophia Loren.

We spent the night dancing, drinking, kissing, and trying to talk to one another over the loud music. As the club was closing down, I grabbed her hand and walked out the door. The other girls were outside waiting, as were my crew. She went over to talk to her friends, then came back to me. She grabbed my hand, and we headed towards our pension. At that point, I wasn't thinking about the owner's 'No Women' policy.

Aurora and I went straight to my bed and began making love all night long. She was beautiful and romantic. I wasn't thinking about my bunk mates either, which was rude, but I was drunk and horny, and she was gorgeous, which usually overrules good bedside manners.

The next morning, the owner entered the room while we were all still asleep and woke us up. She saw Aurora and blew up at me. I thought we would be on the street again, something that wouldn't go down well with my travel mates.

But Aurora spoke to her in Italian, and suddenly her entire attitude changed. The fact that I was with an Italian girl was wonderful to her. She invited the two of us to eat breakfast with her, so we did. All was fine in the world again.

I spent two more glorious days with Aurora, just walking around town, holding hands, and kissing all day long. For the first time, I discovered an international language people with strong feelings for each other can communicate with if they're willing to try. And when that happens, it can be a beautiful experience.

We headed for Rome the next day. Saying goodbye to Aurora on the train platform wasn't easy. I could tell she had fallen for me and I for her. We exchanged addresses, and I told her I would visit her in Sardinia in the future.

My lasting memory of Aurora was there on the train platform, the steam pouring out, wafting around the platform, and we were kissing, saying goodbye. It felt like the scene in "Casablanca" on the train platform when Bogart and Bergman were saying their goodbyes, or at least it felt that way to me.

The train ride to Rome took several hours, which allowed me to catch up on my sleep. We arrived in Rome and spent several days visiting museums, statues, fountains, and other famous landmarks.

I wasn't that interested in museums and the piles of rocks that used to be structures thousands of years ago. I was more interested in the people, culture, and language of a country.

While there, we drank a lot of Italian wine, ate their wonderful food, and looked at their beautiful women. The men and women really do race around on scooters, as is depicted in those old '60s movies like "Roman Holiday."

WILD CHILD

Soon, it was time for Jim to catch his plane for home, so we had one last night of debauchery with him before he flew out the next day. We wished him well and said our farewells as he headed for the major airport in Rome for his flight back to Orange.

Chapter 6

Striking Out on My Own

Bruce, Tim, and I traveled through to Southern Italy, where we took a ship out of Brindisi to the island of Corfu in Greece. I'll always remember that trip because there were some extremely rough seas, and many people got very sick, including Tim. Bruce and I just kept drinking beer, and we turned out perfectly fine.

We exited the ship in Corfu, where we met some American girls. It was cold and raining, and I got very sick with a terrible cough. We ended up riding scooters around the island with the girls, but I wasn't as friendly this time around because of my health. I wasn't in the best shape or mood for several days.

Unfortunately, I chased Bruce and Tim out of the hotel room with my coughing spells, so they went to sleep in the girls' room. Hopefully, I helped them out, and they had a good time. After a few days, I healed up and was ready to get back to having fun.

It was here, though, that Bruce, Tim, and I went our separate ways. They headed off to points unknown, and I headed to the harbor to catch another boat, this time to the port city of Peiraeus, just miles from Athens by bus. It took about a day to get there, but seemed a lot longer since the seas were rough again.

When I got to Athens, I headed for the Plaka and found a cheap hotel called Mary's Place. Bruce and Tim were there, too. I woke up one morning, and they were gone, but it worked out fine for me, as I had been itching to strike out on my own anyway, and now I could. I figured they were headed for Israel, so I spent some time in Athens on my own.

While on the boat from Corfu, I met a young guy from New Jersey named Stew Schneck, who had a lot of family in Israel. He was an actor, a creative type like myself, and we hit it off right away.

Stew invited me to come with him to Israel, so we spent a few more days in Athens and then took a flight to the promised land. When we landed at Ben Gurion Airport in Tel Aviv, I have to admit I was initially a bit thrown with the strong, visible military presence. They were all carrying automatic weapons, and I had never seen anything like it. But I soon got used to it, since the soldiers in their fatigues were on the buses all over the country, carrying automatic weapons.

In Tel Aviv, Stew stayed at his family's house while I bunked at a nearby hotel. We stayed for a few days and headed down south to the Sinai.

Traveling in Israel took time. There was a lot of bus hopping (when you weren't waiting for the various buses), but eventually, Stew and I got off of the bus at a place called Naama Bay and walked down to the beautiful beach there. We set up camp and ended up staying there for about a week, just taking in the sun, even though it was wintertime. We met several Swedish people who were vacationing from their kibbutz.

A week of R & R was just what I needed, as I had picked up a bad case of dysentery in Athens. I needed to just detox on the beach and in the sun. The bay was surrounded by coral caves and cliffs and was gorgeous. I would come down here often during my time in Israel.

Stew and I headed back north one morning, all the way to Kibbutz Shamir, where he had family that were founding members. Shamir was on the Golan Heights border, in the on the finger of Israel in the northern most area of the country.

We woke up early, walked out to the road, and stuck out our thumbs. We figured with the current traffic flow, it would take us few hours to get a ride.

How wrong we were. We were out there all day long until sunset and… no rides. We went back to the beach, had a few beers at the pavilion, and then hit the sack.

We were back at it at the crack of dawn, but after a few hours, it looked like another bad day on the road. One guy who worked at the dive shop kept driving past us on both days. One time he stopped in the road and yelled out to us that maybe we should try smiling, and we might get a ride. Stew and I looked at each other and nodded that he might be right.

We put smiles on our faces and got a ride a few hours later, all the way to Elat. We then took a bus north to Kibbutz Shamir. I had heard of the kibbutzim from Bruce, but I had no idea what they were.

I fell in love with the kibbutz immediately, which is basically a farming community. It's true communism, where everything is communal. They had a small group of European volunteers, mostly from Denmark, who were seasonal workers.

It was just what I was looking for; I told Stew I would stay after I met the head of the kibbutz, Hedva Segal, a young kibbutznik woman who ran the volunteers and seemed to be a kind soul, but the feeling wasn't quite mutual initially.

She was unsure of me because the kibbutz had had many Americans, mostly hippies in the late '60s and early '70s, who took a lot of drugs and smoked pot all the time. I told her I was done with pot, and that was true. She didn't believe me, but let me stay, anyway. She found me a private apartment, and I was thrilled.

Chapter 7

Kibbutz Shamir, Israel

I lived an ideal life on Kibbutz Shamir in the north of Israel. The weather is much like Southern California, sunny for nine months out of the year. I drove around the north of Israel in a jeep wearing shorts, a tank top, and sandals for most of the year and always had a tan. But my tanning wasn't achieved casually by lying on a beach; it came from performing chores on the kibbutz, mostly outdoors.

However, I started in the kitchen for a few weeks with the older kibbutznik women. Most of them didn't speak English, but this was not a stumbling block since I believed you could communicate with anybody if both parties tried. I was the primary dishwasher, but I was also the guy they called on to get all the pots and pans that were up high since I was the tallest person in the kitchen. I worked for a few weeks in the kitchen before moving over to the carpentry shop. I would return to the kitchen from time to time to earn time off to travel around Israel.

After my kitchen duties, I was transferred to the carpentry shop for a short time and then moved to the fish ponds, which became my favorite gig. I loved the job and the people I worked for at the ponds. Most of the time, I worked and hung out with Oded and Vicko, my best friends on the kibbutz; the other person I worked with was Ehckeeam, my boss.

Oded was a Sabra, an Israeli-born citizen. He was a big, gregarious Russian Jew with a booming voice, which is why I nicknamed him Boom Boom. He was a member of Iyala's Garin group that grew up in the Tel Aviv area. His mother lived right off of Dizengoff, the main drag of Tel Aviv, and we spent a lot of time there whenever we were in town.

I met Vicko on his first night at Shamir, and we hit it off immediately. He and I shared some of the same personal histories with drugs. Vicko was born in Egypt and lived in Paris before emigrating to New York City at a young age. He was a city boy who came straight from New York, dressed for the nightlife, which made him stand out a bit. But he soon changed his wardrobe to the standard fashion worn on the kibbutz: jeans and a t-shirt. Soon, he fit in with everybody and felt at home himself.

Ehckeeam was born and raised in Shamir and was a great boss. He was a sports fanatic and would get very emotional during any type of sporting event.

Shamir was founded in 1942 by two groups of Jews from Hungary and Romania who were fleeing war-torn Europe. Kibbutz means "gathering" or "collective" in Hebrew, meaning all the wealth is held in common. A kibbutz is a farming community, but some kibbutzim also have industry operating on them. Shamir, for example, had a very successful lens glass factory. In theory, kibbutzim are similar to what the hippy communes were back in the '60s, but while communes may have been a good idea on paper, in reality, they were rarely successful. By contrast, most kibbutzim throughout Israel were quite successful.

Working on a kibbutz was a lot different from my former job on the docks. I remember one occasion when I was standing on top of the large water tank we used to transport the fish from down the hill (where the fish ponds were) to the top of the hill (where the kibbutz was). We would offload the fish through a funnel into the upper fish tank, where they were then loaded onto the truck for transport to the fish market in Haifa. We did this daily during the season, and I would often drive the tractor to the kibbutz and offload them into the tank. The fish were often sold to the Haifa market, but specific fish meant more for the kibbutzniks, especially on certain holidays.

Ehckeeam, Oded, and Vicko were in the big pond located down the hill in the valley from the kibbutz. They were busy harvesting the fish (in this case, carp) for transport to Scandinavia; apparently, they were big fans of this particular fish.

I had just come up from the pond to switch the tanks and haul the big tank up the hill leading to the kibbutz. It was still early in the morning, our usual time for harvesting the fish. I was heading up the hill with the fish tank and must have fallen asleep because the next thing I knew, I had driven into the ditch on the side of the road.

I looked back and saw that the enormous water tank had nearly fallen on top of me, which would have probably killed me. Instead, it had hit a large rock, then rocked back and forth for a while. But it punctured a large hole in the quarter inch steel. It looked like it had been hit with a missile. Many of the fish were out of the tank and flopping around on the ground.

Once the tractor stopped rocking, I stood up and started yelling down the hill for help. Other workers toiling in the cotton fields nearby in the valley heard me. Soon, everyone within the shouting distance of my voice rushed up the hill to help me.

I was pretty embarrassed by my incompetent driving skills, but nobody said a word about it. Everyone just jumped out of their vehicles and rushed up to me to make sure I was alright, then got busy picking up the fish and throwing them back into the tank. We hooked up one of the cotton tractors to my tractor, and slowly we pulled the tractor and fish tank out of the ditch.

I figured Ehckeeam would have someone else finish driving the fish tank up the hill, but he just looked at me and told me to offload the fish and come back for another load. He wasn't angry or upset with me. I knew if I had made the same mistake at my former job, my boss would've canned me on the spot. But here, everyone, even my boss, was more laid back and even-keeled. No tempers flared, no shouted obscenities, just a "Get-on-with-it" attitude. I loved working under those conditions; it provided a stress-free environment. Maybe that was because there were other reasons to get stressed.

During my stay on Shamir, we were sometimes on high alert because of the threats of attack by the Palestinian Liberation Organization or P.L.O. as it was known then. Because Shamir is near the border of Syria, it was on alert often. Sometimes, the P.L.O. fired missiles into Israel from Lebanon that landed near the kibbutz.

Fortunately, there were enough bomb shelters on the property that provided a haven from the missiles.

Despite the numerous safety measures in place, there were some tragic incidents on Shamir. For example, in 1974, several P.L.O. members snuck on the kibbutz one early morning and invaded the bee house, killing a fifty-six-year-old woman and a pregnant twenty-seven-year-old woman. A young volunteer girl from New Zealand was also killed. She was simply walking to work. In retaliation (and self-defense), the kibbutzniks raided the house and killed all the terrorists. So, while I enjoyed my job hauling fish back and forth from the ponds to the kibbutz, I was always watching the skies and listening for any alarms.

There was a routine to the kibbutz. In the mornings before work began, Eacheeam, Oded, Vicko, and I would drive up to the dining room for coffee, tea, and crackers. We'd work for hours and hours until the work was completed. At night, I was in charge of the volunteer bar. We had splendid music, mixed drinks, and beer. I was chosen to run the bar after only being there a week, but that was because the Englishman that previously ran it had to leave the kibbutz. Addition by subtraction.

I learned to make cocktails; I wasn't exactly a premier bartender, and I'm sure the drinks weren't very good, but everybody drank them anyway. Every Friday night, my friend Naftali let me borrow his record player and records.

I used some of my earned money to buy albums, so we'd have a nice selection of music to listen to and dance to; we had The Doors, Led Zeppelin, The Rolling Stones, Crosby, Stills, Nash, and Young, and many other albums of that ilk. It was a perfect way to spend the night drinking and dancing with friends, enjoying our lives.

That ended when a large group of English volunteers showed up with their disco sensibilities and music, most of it from Saturday Night Fever. Sadly, they ruined our perfect pre-disco, hippy environment.

My most memorable encounter on the kibbutz was with an older fisherman that worked in the ponds for many years. His name was Solomon, and he was a huge man with a big heart. Sadly, his son had been killed in the '73 Yom Kippur War, and it broke that big heart of his, from which he never fully recovered.

He took me under his wing, and for a few days a week, he helped me begin my journey of learning Hebrew. I wanted to learn the ancient language not just for myself but for Iyala.

Solomon had an amazing past; he was one of the founders of Israel. He used to joke that he had done "some sailing" off the Israeli coast in the Mediterranean Sea. I later discovered that Solomon was actually one of the Jews that ran the British blockades in old ships to bring war-torn Jewish refugees to their new homeland when the country was just getting started. This was an incredibly dangerous endeavor that he undertook as the British would, ram the old ships or force them into port and expel everyone on board from Palestine (as Israel was then known).

To further my Hebrew lessons, I enrolled in the Ulpan school for Hebrew in kiryat Shemona. It was established in the early days of Israel's state to teach Hebrew to the many immigrants pouring in from all over the planet. They taught the basics of grammar and vocabulary, and then you went out into the streets to practice and learn. I wasn't that fluent, but the teachers taught me enough to get by. When I was traveling through Europe, I would write Iyala letters in Hebrew. Over the years, I've retained my Hebrew-speaking abilities but can no longer read or write in Hebrew. Some lessons never end; you just have to continue to learn.

Chapter 8

Iyala

And, of course, there was Iyala, my Israeli girlfriend. She was 19, and I was 22. Iyala was tall, about 5'7", with thin long arms and legs, dark black curly hair, and a beautiful face with sharp features with large, almond-shaped dark eyes and sun-kissed olive skin. What an exotic beauty. But those weren't her best features. What made me really fall in love with her was her heart and soul, her gentle nature, and her outlook on life. She helped take the edge off me, and we were madly in love and did most everything together.

We met soon after I arrived at the kibbutz. I was coming back from a hike with some volunteers, including Naftali, our kibbutznik guide, on the field trip. I had only been at the kibbutz for a few days, but I already loved it.

We were walking up the hill from the volunteer ghetto (as it was known) when I first laid eyes on Iyala. She was beautiful, yes, but there was something in her eyes and in my gut that told me yes. Even though she also had this look in her eyes that said 'Stay away from me, Mr. California.' I thought, in my youthful cockiness, 'Not a chance!' And BAM, it was the proverbial love at first sight.

I'd see her around the kibbutz, mainly in the dining room at night, but she was always surrounded by the young men and women of her Army group, the Garin. I didn't want to rush it, anyway. She was doing Israeli folk dancing, so right away, I put that on my "To Learn" list (which I did, and it was fun). Guys will do just about anything to get into a woman's heart. Still, like most guys, once Iyala and I were together, I gave up on trying to impress her because it wasn't necessary with Iyala, and I never danced folk dancing again.

Her childhood friend was Hedva, who was also in the Garin. She worked in the kitchen with me, so we had many chances to chat and get to know one another. Like many volunteers who first arrive on the kibbutz, we were put to work in the kitchen. It was a rite of passage, similar to the young Japanese men who showed up at Samurai school expecting to become Samurai overnight; they were immediately told to report to the kitchen to wash dishes for three years. Most of the young men left the school when they learned that was their job, but the ones who made it through learned the first lesson of being a Samurai: Patience.

One Friday, Hedva approached me. She had sensed that I had a huge crush on Iyala. She offered to teach me Hebrew so that I could talk to Iyala. I smiled because I thought I was harboring a secret, but women have that gift of being able to see right through us. I said, sure, why not! Hedva taught me two very important questions: *"Do you want to dance with me?"* and *"Do you want to come with me?"* Little did I realize how magical those two little questions would be in my young life.

I walked into the volunteer bar about 8 p.m. on a Friday, and the place was already pretty full. I ordered a Gold Star, my favorite Israeli beer, and sat down at the bar. I looked around, not recognizing many people, but I saw Iyala and her Garin friends at a table near the front.

After a few more beers, I started glancing in Iyala's direction. She and I seemed to be stealing quick looks at one another; there was electricity in the air. I waited for a good song to come on before I'd walk over to try out my beginning Hebrew.

Soon, "Brown Sugar" by The Rolling Stones came on. I finished my beer and set it down on the bar. Then, I got up and walked towards Iyala. But as I got close, one of her male friends, Hiam, got up and tried to block me from her. I stopped and stared at him to see what his next move would be. But Iyala said something to him in Hebrew, and he sat back down. Hiam turned out to be Iyala's recent ex-boyfriend.

I walked up, opened my mouth, and asked her in my new Hebrew, *"Aut rosaut learcold etee?"* (*"Do you want to dance with me?"*) Her face lit up, and she smiled that beautiful smile of hers and said, *"Ken"* (*"Yes"*). I extended my hand. She took it, and we walked out onto the dance floor. I was in heaven. We danced all night.

Toward the end of the night, the bar was thinning out and getting ready to close. I thought it was time to try my other Hebrew phrase. The music was loud, so I leaned in and said, *"Aut rosaut lavoh etee?"* (*"Do you want to come with me?"*). She laughed again and said, *"Ken"* (*"Yes"*).

We held each other's hands and walked out of the bar, all the way followed by the harsh stares of her Garin group. My apartment was around the corner from the bar, but I was in no rush to be with her, so I asked her where she lived so I could walk her home. As she spoke little English, and I certainly didn't speak Hebrew, it took a while for her to understand that I was going to walk her home.

By coincidence, she also lived close to the bar, so it only took a few minutes to get to her apartment. We stood there for a few moments; then, I leaned down, and we kissed for the first time. We kissed and kissed and kissed. Eventually, she opened the door, and we walked in, continuing our mutual affection. Neither of us meant for it to happen, nor did we plan it, but we stayed up most of the night making love and talking as best we could.

We woke up the next morning, still struggling to talk to each other. The first thing Iyala said in her broken English was, "What would my mother say if she saw me now?" I smiled. I was already smitten with her, and I believed she reciprocated that feeling.

Within a few days, I moved in with her, and we were officially a couple. Of course, it was a shock to most people on the kibbutz, as I was a white non-Jewish volunteer. But I soon became fast friends with most of her Garin group and many of the kibbutzniks.

But this "opposites attract" scenario was nothing new. It was an age-old story on the kibbutz that a young kibbutznik falls for a foreign volunteer; then the volunteer leaves, saying they will come back, but they never do, and the kibbutznik is left broken-hearted.

Life with Iyala in the kibbutz was beautiful. We were madly in love. I worked in the fish ponds, ran the bar, and made many friends, both kibbutzniks, and volunteers. I've often thought that I could have easily lived my entire life there.

Iyala and I would communicate mainly in English since she knew more English than I knew Hebrew. At times, we had an interpreter. Iyala's friend, Coates, had an apartment next to hers. Occasionally, when I would ramble on, Iyala would signal for me to wait. Then she'd run next door to Coates' apartment and repeat what I said, asking what I meant. He'd tell her then Iyala would run back and answer me. But this only lasted for a few weeks; she was remembering her English from school and was getting better and better with it. I loved this beginning period of our relationship. Finally, we were speaking in that romantic international language.

However, my relationship with Iyala was not without its difficulties, especially off of the kibbutz. After all, we were an interracial couple, and interracial couples have difficulties everywhere in the world. It was more pronounced living in Israel. Iyala was dark-skinned, and I was white. She was Jewish, and I was a Christian, goyim (the Hebrew term for a non-Jewish person).

To complicate matters, Iyala's father was a very religious man. But over time, I think he came to respect me as a hardworking man who made his daughter happy; however, since I wasn't Jewish, his religious beliefs couldn't accept me as a future husband for his daughter.

Away from the kibbutz, people would look at us with crossed eyes and whisper. Once on a bus, a dark-skinned soldier said to Iyala in Hebrew, *"Lama who?" ("Why him?")*. I understood enough Hebrew to understand him. Iyala said something to him in Hebrew. I started to get up, but when Iyala saw me, she quickly asked me not to.

On the positive side, Iyala's three siblings accepted me. However, her brother, Iya, said to me once, *"Why not just convert to Hebrew and make the old man happy?"* I told him it was a tough decision; on some days, I'd wake up believing I could go through with it, while on other days, I'd wake up and realized I couldn't.

At that time in my life, I was somewhere between an atheist and an agnostic, and I had a hard time accepting anyone's religion, let alone converting to another religion I didn't believe.

If I decided to convert, I'd have to do it in Jerusalem with an ultra-orthodox Rabbi instead of a reformed Rabbi back home in the States. That meant I would be going to school six days a week, for six to nine months. In the end, I'd probably know more about Judaism than most other Jews in the world. But that was a question I didn't want or need to answer at that time in my life.

Chapter 9

Getting Ready to Head Back Out onto the Road Again

I had been on Shamir for about six months now and thought it was time for me to get back on the road. But, unfortunately, Iyala couldn't leave the kibbutz for two reasons. First was that she wasn't finished with her military service, and the other was the more serious issue of her religion.

I planned on returning to Europe for a little while and cruise around, nothing serious; I knew I was coming back in six months. I needed to let everyone on the kibbutz know of my pending departure. By this time, I was friendly with both the kibbutzniks and the volunteers, so Iyala and I had a small party with the younger kibbutzniks, which was a ton of fun. We did what kibbutzniks often do, sat around outside on the grass, drinking tea and coffee while playing music. Most of Iyala's Garin group and many of the young kibbutzniks showed up. I went to the bar and got a case of beer for everybody.

Of course, Vicko, and Oded were there. I took an extra-large, white t-shirt and drew the name BOOM BOOM across the front in Peter Max-type lettering and gave it to him that night. He loved it and put it on. Many of us stayed out late that night, just being together, enjoying each other's company, and having a good time. It made for a nice memory.

Iyala and I decided to head down to Naama Bay at the bottom of the Sinai Peninsula near Sharm el-Sheikh. It was still a part of Israel then. Naama means "pleasure," and it was. It was a beautiful bay with only a dive shop, a small hotel, a pavilion, and a palm-thatched restaurant. Virtually untouched. Now under Egypt, it looks like Waikiki Beach with all the high-rise hotels.

We decided to stay at the youth hostel in Sharm el-Sheikh a few miles down the road instead of camping on the beach. I figured I would have plenty of outdoor camping soon, so a bed, for now, would be extra nice.

We spent several days there, hanging out on the beach, walking around, and talking a lot. It was the end of spring, hot and cloudless all day long. We went swimming often. One day off the tip of Sharm el-Sheikh, we ended up making love in the water. However, I scraped my leg against a coral reef and ended up with a bad infection on my leg that lasted for several weeks.

On the way back to Shamir, we stopped by Kibbutz Dorot in the Negev Desert to visit Bruce and Tim. My Mother told me where they were staying, having spoken to Bruce's Mom.

Iyala and I stayed there for a couple of days. We partied with Bruce, Tim, and their friends. Iyala didn't drink, but that night she tried smoking pot for the first time. She took several hits and got quite baked, so I spent the night taking care of her. That was it for her and pot.

We got back to Shamir a couple of days before I was to leave the country. As I had already completed my job duties, I spent the rest of my time roaming the kibbutz, saying goodbye to friends. I would leave Haifa via a cruise ship that constantly ran between Haifa, the Greek Isles, and Athens, Greece.

On my last night with Iyala, we ate in our apartment. We were going to spend the night alone, just talking and being together. So we put on some music, ate our dinner, and talked through the night.

We talked about our future lives together, what we would do, and where we would live, Israel or America. She knew I wanted to be an actor and that there wouldn't be much work for me in Israel. We talked about living in both countries, our optimum plan.

We also talked about our relationship while we were apart. Would we be loyal to each other, or would we experience other people? I told her I planned to marry her when I came back and spend my life with her. I didn't want to be forty years old and have her decide she wanted to experience other people because when we met, she was so young and hadn't had the opportunity to do that. I told her I thought she should have fun, have a few flings with other men, as it would be her last chance to have that experience, and I, in turn, would do the same.

Iyala and I left Shamir by bus the morning of my departure. We went straight to Haifa, where the boat was docked. We had some time to kill, so we just hugged and talked until the boat began loading passengers.

We kissed, and I promised Iyala that I would be returning. I waved to her from the deck of the ship. It was the hardest departure I ever had, and I thought hard about getting off the ship, forgetting about my trip, grabbing ahold of Iyala, and never letting her go.

But that didn't happen. I decided to go through with the rest of my trip, knowing that I would, one day, return to the love of my life.

Chapter 10

The Greek Isles

Instead of going straight to Athens, I cruised the Greek Isles. My first stop was Crete; I'd be there for some time. Thankfully, it was an uneventful trip. I found a space on the boat's deck and settled into a good book for the trip over. Ironically, the book I was reading at the time was "Exodus" by Leon Uris.

I departed the ship and headed to the main road that led to the beach at the other end of the island. I figured I'd hitchhike my way across the island, stopping off at different historical sites along the way. Unfortunately, hitchhiking was tough on the island, so I ended up doing a lot of walking and, when I got tired, busing. As I was in no hurry, I arrived at the beach a few days later.

I walked along the beach and found a secluded spot to set up camp. I did not know how long I'd be staying. I left it up to the Fates; whatever happened would happen. Que Sera Sera. Walking on the beach, I met a small group of young American vacationers, a couple of older Dutch women, and another young man from Ireland.

We hung out for a few days. It was my birthday, and the others threw a party for me. They drew a picture of me surfing and called it "King Tracy." They all signed it, and I still have it. We drank a lot of ouzo that night in front of the fire, dancing and listening to music.

I left the beach a few days later with the two Dutch girls; they had a car and were going my way past the harbor. I got on the cruise ship, heading for the Isle of Ios for the first time. It would later become my favorite island, one that I would visit many times over. As it is one of the smaller Greek Isles, Ios doesn't get as crowded as the other larger ones.

As soon as I got off the boat, I noticed the bright, beautifully colored homes that adorn the hillside. On the way over, I met a guy named Steve. He was from Colorado and seemed like a good guy, so we hung out for a while, checking out the scenery; then we headed to the beach to find a campsite.

The next day, while walking on the beach by myself, a young blond girl shouted out for me to come over to their camp, so I headed over. The young blond girl's name was Carol, and she was from Oregon. I ended up spending several hours there with her and her friends. We sat around listening to two guys playing guitar and drinking ouzo and orange soda, a nice combination.

Carol and I hooked up for a few days; one night, we went to a club in town, dancing the night away. After too much ouzo, we ended up in an empty field, making love all night in the dirt. We parted ways after just a few short days because I wasn't through with my island hopping.

From Ios, I traveled to Mykonos, a very popular and crowded island. Next up was Rhodes, one of the largest Greek islands, very busy and very crowded. Steve had heard of a secluded beach a couple of miles from the harbor, so we got off the boat and headed there.

Once there, we set up camp and met a couple of guys from South Africa, Hans, and Mikael. We hung out for the next couple of days on this essentially private beach and lagoon and became fast friends with our new beach mates.

On the third day, two young women from Switzerland joined us, Renata and Gertrude. Renata and I hit it off immediately; I didn't know it then, but she would play an important role in my life over the next few years.

By now, my daily life had become an exotic routine. I hung out with my newfound friends, swam, read, sat in the sun, talked about everything under the sun, listened to live music (someone always had a guitar), drank ouzo, and partied all night; all the while surrounded by beautiful island scenery and women. Not a bad life for a young man like me, if you can get it.

One day, Renata told me she was leaving for Mykonos. So I left, too. I told her my next destination was Samos, an island with beautiful mountains and beaches close to the Turkish coast. I figured I could catch a fishing boat to Turkey from there.

We agreed to meet in Samos in two weeks. We stayed up most of the night talking and making love wherever and whenever we could. We left the next day, going in our separate directions.

On the boat to Samos, I met three American travelers who had just come back from China, which had just opened up to tourists. They were a couple, Brian, and Linda, and a single woman, Siena, and like so many strangers I'd met on this trip, we all became fast friends. They had been in China for several months studying acupressure.

They were going to Samos to stay with some friends, Sean, an Irishman, and Shelly, an English gal, who had a home there; and Erma, an Australian gal, who was also staying with them. Sean was one of the founding members of Greenpeace, and Shelly was his wife and a great cook. Erma was a bat shit crazy gal and a wild child, which I loved.

I really loved Samos. It's off the beaten path, and many Greeks consider it their favorite island. We stayed at Shelly's house for a couple of days and then headed to a beach on the backside of the island that Sean said was beautiful and almost abandoned, except for the local fisherman.

It was a long hike from the road, so we took our time. And Sean was right; it was beautiful. We set up camp as the sun was setting. We started a campfire. Sean pulled out some homemade ouzo made by a little old man that rode his donkey around the island, smashed all day long on his own product.

The next day was a relaxing one; I was reading a new book, which turned out to be popular with my new group of friends. It was "Even Cowgirls Get the Blues" by Tom Robbins. That night we drank more ouzo and smoked a lot of pot. Erma, Siena, and I were sitting down at the water's edge in silence, smoking pot on a foggy, full moonlit night.

Then something happened that I had only heard or read about but had never seen with my own eyes. I was looking up at the sky when suddenly, I saw an object, or a light, zoom in to view a couple of hundred feet off the beach and a couple of hundred feet above the water. It hovered there, swaying back and forth for several minutes, and then zoomed off into the distance, gone in a flash.

I had never seen anything move that quickly, and I grew up on Marine air bases watching fast jets flying. I just sat there in stoned silence, unsure of what I had just witnessed.

I looked around at the girls on either side of me, and they had the same bewildered look on their faces. And almost simultaneously, we all said, *"Did you see that"?* After a brief discussion, we went back to smoking pot in silence.

Was it the pot? I don't think so. So my only conclusion was that it was some secret military aircraft (though it was too quick for that) or an alien spacecraft. I'll never know.

One day, I went to the post office to pick up a letter from Renata that she said she'd leave for me. We had agreed to meet up on Samos, and I was looking forward to hearing from her. I arrived at the post office, but there was no letter. I figured she changed her mind. Too bad. I liked her.

I stayed another two days and, as most of us were leaving Shelly prepared a great meal for our last night there. It was a combination of the local seafood and vegetables. What a feast!

We exchanged contact information and said our goodbyes. Then, I headed for the harbor to find the fishing boat to Turkey, admittedly a country I knew little about at that point, but it sounded exotic and fascinating, so off I went.

I was a little suspicious of taking a fishing boat into the country, believing it may be illegal on some level, but I went for it, anyway. So I found the boat, paid my fee, and off we went.

En route, I met an American couple, and they told me about a new movie that had just opened back home, "Midnight Express." It was about a young American guy arrested at the Istanbul airport for trying to smuggle out a lot of hash. He spent several years in a Turkish prison until he escaped.

They gave me an American newspaper to read. There was a review of the film, so I read it, and it got into my head; to be honest, it made me paranoid. I quickly searched my backpack and threw everything overboard that looked suspicious; herbs and everything. I wasn't taking any chances.

We landed at Dimim, a small port, and fishing village on the coast near Izmir. I hitchhiked there, taking a few days until I reached the highway near Aydin.

But again, I wasn't in any rush to get anywhere. I arrived in Izmir on the eve of Ramadan, the high holy holiday for Muslims that lasted a month; it comprised fasting during the day from sun up to sundown and feasting at night.

Of course, I knew nothing about this at the time. The next morning at sunrise, I was awakened by the sound of savage drums pounding outside my hotel room that scared the shit out of me. The drums were marking the beginning of Ramadan and fasting for the day. I had checked into a hotel in the afternoon the day before, wanting to get some good sleep for a few days. But that was not to be.

That day, I met another western traveler who was also headed to Istanbul. Her name was Camille, and she was a beautiful blonde from Paris. We traveled together to Istanbul.

That night, we went out for some beers at a western-style bar that looked right out of the Old West. After several beers, I was getting a little drunk. Then, four Turkish men came to the table to introduce themselves to us. They had been checking us out from across the room. I wondered what their game was and figured it was Camille.

They bought us beers for the next few hours, and by then, I was really drunk. Then it dawned on me. A moment of clarity. I realized Camille wasn't their target after all. Camille realized it at the same time as I did, and we both just looked at each other and started laughing.

I figured it was time to leave, so I said goodbye and got up to leave. They let us know right away that that didn't work for them. They assumed (wrongly) they had paid for my ass and were hellbent to collect. Realizing this, Camille and I made our way to the exit and left with them close on our tails.

WILD CHILD

We started running and laughing all the way back to our hotel. Unfortunately, the large doors were closed when we got there. We banged loudly on them, our new amorous best friends close behind on our heels.

The hotel manager opened the doors, and in pidgin English, we somehow got him to understand our plight. He grabbed what looked like a cricket bat and started yelling at them, eventually chasing them away. Finally, he came back and started bawling us out, I think. Camille and I then retreated to our rooms for some much-needed sleep.

The next day, I didn't feel like hitchhiking, and neither did Camille, so instead, we got on a bus to Istanbul, where Camille boarded a plane back to Paris.

I found my way to Lyle's Pudding Shop near Sultan Mohammad Square and the Blue Mosque, a major hangout for western travelers as old Constantinople was the east and west axis points. I spent a lot of time at Lyle's during my years on the road.

I toured the city with the new friends I met and fell in love with the Grand Bazaar. It was a place I'd spend much time over the years doing small business deals. Everything is a negotiation in this part of the world; it was here and in Jerusalem where I lost my business virginity.

Lyle's was also the first place where I heard about running cars from west to east for money. I met a Dutch gentleman who had just driven a car while traveling to India from Munich. He told me to go to the main train station in Munich, and I'd know who the players were by sight. I thought that was a useful piece of information, so I stored it away for the future.

Chapter 11

A Gigolo

One day, I looked at a map of Europe and had an idea that sounded good to me. I dipped my finger in a cup of water, closed my eyes, held my hand over the map, making a circle above it; wherever the drop of water landed, from my hand to the map would be my next destination. It was totally random using my moist hand as a geographical divining rod. Silly as it seems now, back then, I decided this would be my new way of making my travel plans. Fortunately, the drop landed near Nice in the south of France. I would head there the next day.

Once again, I wasn't feeling up to hitchhiking, so I grabbed a bus to Milan, Italy. It was a two-day drive, but that was fine with me; I could use the downtime to catch up on sleep and reading. Traveling through Bulgaria and Yugoslavia into Italy was one of my favorite trips, and I had a perfect view right out of my large bus window of the beautiful countryside.

The bus arrived in Milan early in the morning, and instead of sightseeing, I headed for the highway to start my voyage to Nice. It was summer and a beautiful day for bumming a ride.

The Hitchhiking Gods were smiling down on me this day. Almost immediately, a young guy in his early thirties driving a convertible 911 Porsche pulled over and told me to hop in, so I did. He was an Italian named Giovanni, and he was heading to Cannes, just down the road from Nice. One ride for the total trip? Pretty damn good.

The ride was fun; we stopped on the way for a few beers and to smoke some hash Giovanni had brought with him. The sun was out;

the top was down; the wind was blowing, and the music was playing. It was a beautiful trip, all in all.

When we arrived in Nice, Giovanni pulled over to the side of the road, looked at me, and asked if I wanted to make some good money. I smiled and told him I didn't play that way. He laughed and said, "Neither, did he." That was not what he was meant. He told me he was a gigolo and that if I cleaned myself up and bought some nice clothes, I'd make a killing along the hotels and casinos of the French Riviera.

He told me about his experiences over several years of doing it and how he lived a luxurious lifestyle because of it. He traveled the planet like I did, only via private planes and luxury yachts.

He told me his "clients" were mostly older women who were divorced or widowed. They were looking for young, handsome men to be a part of their lives: traveling, accompanying them in public (arm in arm, naturally), and making love to them. He said that many of these women knew what they were doing in bed.

Giovanni then said he'd float me some money so I could clean myself up and buy some new Italian clothes. He even said I could stay at his apartment in Cannes. I told him I needed some time to think about his offer.

He agreed and said to let him know. He said we'd have a blast traveling the world together since many of these women hung out in small groups. He handed me his business card and said I hope you join me on this adventure. I hopped out and said I was definitely going to think about it.

Chapter 12

Bully on the Beach

After walking through downtown Nice, I made my way down to the beautiful beach. Several young people camping along the wall separated the beach from the boardwalk and the city.

I set up camp across from a small group and started reading. A young Frenchman walked up, and we started talking. His name was Andre; he was from the Brittany region in the northern part of France. Like me, he was roaming the planet, and like others before him, Andre became my new hangout buddy. Amid Andre's group was a big German that was camping next to us.

He was loud and obnoxious, bragging about his life as a thief; in his German-accented English, he went on about what he had stolen, which neither bothered nor impressed me. The problem was, he kept it up. He wouldn't shut up. Instead, he started acting like the big dog, bullying and belittling the others in the camp, picking on them, and even threatening them with physical violence. All the while, he continued playing with a big knife, waving it around. I could see he and I were headed for an old-fashioned showdown.

One afternoon, I had enough. I got up, walked over to where the big German was, and started packing up his belongings. He asked me what I was doing, but I said nothing; I just kept packing his stuff until I was done.

I then walked over to him, got in his space, and quietly stared at him. He went silent, but I could tell he was nervous since I was as big as he was. I said, *"You're leaving now."* I had watched too many Clint

Eastwood movies as a kid. He put his hand on his knife, but I just kept staring at him.

This went on for a while until he flinched. He backed up and started stuttering in a high-pitched voice. He then walked over, picked up his stuff, and headed up the stairs towards the boardwalk, disappearing over the edge. A few of the young travelers came up and quietly thanked me.

After I did my good deed, Andre and I went to town to get some fresh bread, Camembert cheese, and some wine. We returned to the beach, devoured the bread and cheese and sipped the wine all night long. I mean, when in France, you know. Clint would have approved.

Chapter 13

Sur le Pont d'Avignon

I spent a few weeks alternating between small towns and villages to larger cities. I wanted to soak in the different atmospheres each of them offered. I decided to look for work as my funds were getting low; I knew that the grape harvest was beginning soon, but I needed to find a temporary job first.

One night, I ended up in a small town looking for a place to sleep when I came to a park. I saw a young couple there and asked them if it was cool to sleep here. The guy said in a heavy Cockney accent, "Sure, mate."

They invited me to sit down with them. As it turned out, they weren't a couple after all; the girl had arrived not long before me. Soon after I came on the scene, she got up, said goodbye, and left.

The Cockney's name was Liam, and he was from London but spoke fluid French, something I was trying to learn. I had a book on learning French, "Hugo's French in Three Months," and I was desperately studying it, trying to figure it out. If people see you struggling to speak their language, they will usually help you out.

Being a Cockney, Liam was born within the sound of Bow Bells in East London. He and I hit it off right away and conversed all night. Like me, he was looking for work and suggested we find a job picking fruit until the grape harvest began. That sounded good to me, so we made a plan for the next morning to hit the road and look for a job.

We hitchhiked to Avignon and cruised around the city. That night, we set up camp close to the city's historic bridge. It was built of wood in the 1100s, and parts of the original bridge still existed. There is a beautiful children's song about it, "Sur le Pont d'Avignon," though that night wasn't so beautiful for us.

We set up camp and got to sleep early; I secured my backpack with straps and used it as my pillow, as was my custom. Just as the sun was showing itself, I awoke to the sounds of voices and footsteps. I reached under my backpack for my knife. I looked up just in time to get kicked in the eye. It jerked my head back and left me dazed for a few moments.

When my head cleared, the first thing I noticed was that my knife was still in my hand. Someone was kneeling on me and had a knife to my throat. I looked around and saw another man atop Liam with a knife to his throat. But that man had a stocking over his head, the only one wearing a disguise. A third man grabbed my backpack; he was trying to open it, but my securing job was working, and in the early morning light, he couldn't open it.

The thieves were yelling at each other in Arabic; they seemed very nervous. I thought I could pull my knife out and drive my 6 inch blade into the crotch of the man on me; then, I would quickly crossover to the man trying to open my backpack and stick him in his ribs.

But that would leave Liam's guy to deal with, and I knew I couldn't be quick enough to get to him before he cut Liam's throat. Besides, I had maybe $50 on me, and it wasn't worth it possibly to harm or kill someone over so little money.

I made sure to take a few conscious notes. One, the man on me was the leader. Two, he had the backside of the blade to my neck. Three, they were pushing me physically to open my backpack up, which I refused. And four, the man that was on Liam was very nervous and had the actual blade of the knife to Liam's throat. I could see droplets of blood.

Liam was yelling at me in his Cockney accent, "Open the focking bag, you focking cunt!" but I refused. I yelled back at Liam, "No!" We went back and forth for a bit, but when I looked into the eyes of the man that had the blade to Liam's throat and saw no intelligence but more blood, I gave in and opened my bag.

They found the $50 I had and took my watch off my wrist. Then they grabbed my passport, but I quickly snatched it back. I pulled my knife out and pushed the man that was on me off. I stood up and held my knife out towards them, ready to go.

We looked at each other for a few moments, then the leader said something to the other two in Arabic, and they ran off into the night. Liam was pissed off at me until we both started laughing, albeit with a very nervous laugh.

We couldn't get back to sleep, so we got up, broke camp, and headed into town. Just as we were leaving the waterside camp, a man dropped from a nearby tree with his backpack. He had slept in the tree all night. It was an excellent idea and safer than sleeping out in the open. It was something I would store away for later.

I wanted to find the thieves who robbed us, but there were too many Muslim men in the cafes and around town; I couldn't distinguish them from the ones that had robbed us, and rather than punish an innocent civilian, I decided to let the incident go.

As Liam and I walked the streets, I noticed the cafes were already full; there were already many people walking the streets. We had just turned down an alleyway when I saw a 50 franc note blowing down towards me. What luck! The Universe provides. I picked it up and showed it to Liam. We became ecstatic since, by this time, we were both starving.

We sat down at an outdoor café and ordered some croissants, tea, and coffee. While waiting for our food, I noticed an older couple walking down the sidewalk. I noted them because they held hands and looked at each other; clearly, they were still madly in love even after all those years together. It reminded me of Iyala and what I hoped we would be like in future years to come.

The old man pulled his hand out of his pocket, and a bill fell out of his pocket and landed on the ground. I got up to retrieve it and give it back to him, but I froze when I saw it was another 50 franc note. I kept the bill instead of giving it back to him. I felt bad about keeping it and still do, to this day. But I justified it by thinking (and believing) that this was the Universe's way of paying me back. Liam and I had nearly lost our lives to a couple of common thieves who had taken everything of value from us, and now we were getting reimbursed.

In retrospect, though, I desperately needed the money. I realize now I should have given it back to the couple. Though I'm not terribly religious in my beliefs or philosophy, I believe in Karma. This was a test… and I failed it. The consequences of my failure would show up in time; I was sure of that. But that morning, all I thought about was survival. Liam and I ate heartily.

Chapter 14

Picking Fruit

I had been thinking about Giovani's invitation to join him on his journey as a gigolo, especially after being robbed. But I also thought that it wasn't my thing; I just couldn't bring myself to do that, become a kept man. I decided to put it away for the time being.

Liam and I headed for the countryside to find work picking fruit; we stopped at several farms along the way, but no one was hiring. However, one farmer told us about a large farm that hired many fruit pickers. It was in a small town north of where we were called Bagnols-sur-Cèze.

We hitchhiked to the town and stopped at a café to ask for directions and get some warm croissants. They told us the farm was located a few kilometers just up the road we were on. We ate our croissants, drank our coffee and hot chocolate, and then headed up the road. We walked, something you do a lot of when traveling by thumb and backpack.

We found the farm and went straight to the main office; we were hired right away. They provided a bunkhouse for their workers, which was near full capacity. Luckily, Liam and I procured a room just for us. Most of the workers were a mixture of Moroccan Muslims and young locals looking for work during their summer break.

Our boss was a short, round, cheerful man in his 30s with a short, round wife and five little round children. He wore the blue dungaree uniform of a socialist and was always smiling.

WILD CHILD

I soon discovered that we could earn extra money by exceeding your daily quota of apples. It was an easy motivation for me to work harder; I even worked on one of my days off because I wanted to make enough extra money to call Iyala by phone at the end of the month. My boss would speak to me in French, telling me to slow down. He would say slow, slow with his expressive hands, as in life is too short.

I let Iyala know I would call her on a certain day and time so she could receive the call. I kept up my furious work ethic every weekday and Saturday.

After a week, we got a new roommate named Henri, a young Frenchman who wanted to make some extra money before going into the Army to perform his mandatory military service.

He only spoke French, so I couldn't communicate with him well, but Liam could. I practiced my French with him and others by using my book and insisting that they all speak only French to me.

I wrote a lot of letters in the evenings. I wrote Renata, whom I met in Greece in the summer, as soon as I arrived there but never heard from her.

All my mail caught up with me while I was on the farm. This was a blessing because I was rarely in one place long enough to get my mail, and by now, I was receiving several months of mail all at once.

A couple of young pickers owned stamp collections, so I gave them the envelopes to take home, and they'd peel off the stamps and bring the envelopes back to me.

Chapter 15

The Red, the Red, the Woman in Red

After a few weeks, I was showering one night after a long day of work. Suddenly, Henri rushed into the room. He was very excited, shouting at me in French, waving his arms and yelling, *"Le rouse, le rouse, la femme en rouse!" ("The red, the red, the woman in red!")*. I wasn't sure exactly what he meant, but since Henri was never one to get that excited, I dried off and followed him to find out what drove him to such a state.

I walked into our room, and there stood Renata with her flaming red hair. She and a tall young man were talking to Liam. It shocked me to see her here. As it turned out, she had received my letter, but instead of writing back, she drove here to see me. She was heading to her other home in the south of France, a small village named Salernes, and wanted me to come with her for a few weeks.

Renata said she had enough money for both of us, but I just couldn't do that. I thought hard about it, but told her I couldn't since I was still broke and needed more money. She tried to talk me into it. Everyone did, including Liam and Henri, but I stuck to my guns. I was raised to make my own way and not live off of another person.

We all went down to the local café for a drink. The young man with Renata was her younger brother, Claude. After several drinks, we got a bit drunk. Liam, though, got so drunk, he started arguing with Renata and Claude about Switzerland's role in World War Two. I was appalled at his rudeness. They argued back and forth for a while until I told Liam to knock it off.

WILD CHILD

With that brief episode over, Renata and Claude tried again to get me to go with them, but I already made my stubborn mind up. I told her I'd head over to Zurich to see her when I finished working on the grapes. We then drove back to our bunkhouse. Admittedly, it was hard to say goodbye to Renata, but I did.

The next day Liam and Henri told everyone about my decision, and even my little boss came up to me and shook his head as if to say 'Crazy American.'

Two days later, we were in our room eating spaghetti that Liam had made. I was eating it from the pot he had cooked it in when Renata walked in. She had driven back up from her home to try to convince me for the last time to come with her.

I looked at her, then over at Liam and Henri. I needed no more convincing. I quickly got up, grabbed my clothes, and left without saying a word to the applause of Henri and Liam.

On the way, we stopped at some Swiss friends of hers that lived in France. They had a vineyard and made their own wine. Renata bought a few cases to take home to Zurich.

We arrived at her home in this small, quaint cobblestone village. Her home was a two-story structure on a street that came to a Y intersection. The home had been owned by a family of shoe cobblers that had lived there for hundreds of years, and there were still old cobbler tools left behind in storage.

There was a large loft in the main room, with a separate, small living room, and bedroom. That was where we slept, while Claude slept on the couch downstairs.

We worked on the home during the day and relaxed and talked at night. We stayed there for three weeks until it was time for Renata and Claude to get back to work. We packed up, locked up, and drove back to my work first. We said our goodbyes. As I had promised her before, I told Renata I'd see her in Zurich in the late fall when the grape harvest ended.

I headed into the bunkhouse, where I found Liam and Henri eating lunch. They were both happy to see me. They asked how it went with Renata. I told them about her cool home and what a great time we had.

It was time to go back to work, but I needed to change clothes, so they left ahead of me. After changing, I headed toward the orchards to find the picking crew.

I saw them standing around, and when I walked up, they broke out into applause for me. My boss walked up and hugged me as if to say, 'That's the way you live life!' I thought for certain that I'd be fired, and if this were America, I would have been, but not in the south of France.

The next Saturday was my scheduled call to Iyala, and I was looking forward to it. Time seemed to crawl by slowly. But finally, the day came, and I left work early and made my way to the office. Because it was an international call, I had to use one of the office phones. My boss set me up in an office by myself so that I would have some privacy.

I made the call, and Iyala answered the phone in the kibbutz dining room. It was so good to hear her voice. I asked her simply to talk to me because all I wanted to hear was her voice. We ended up talking for close to an hour about my trip and what everyone was doing on the kibbutz. The time flew by, but I needed to hang up, as it was costing me a lot of money. I told her I'd be back around the beginning of the year and told her I loved her and said goodbye.

One Sunday afternoon, Liam and I were hitchhiking and got dropped off at a highway entrance where two French girls were also hitchhiking. We walked up and started talking with them. Their names were Genevieve and Delphine. They were both in their early 20s. Genevieve was a small, thin girl who seemed drawn to Liam; the feeling was mutual. Delphine was more my type, and luckily for me, I seemed to be hers too. Delphine was medium height with dark eyes, long dark hair, and a great body and friendly soul, I would find out.

We split up into couples to hitchhike back to Bagnols-sur-Cèze; coincidentally, the girls were from there. We became close for the next few weeks and spent most of our free time with them. Delphine told me she would head to London in a month to begin a year-long contract as a nanny for a rich English couple. We knew then we would only have a short time together, and we made the most of it. It was a brief but intense relationship.

WILD CHILD

We worked on the farm for a few more weeks and then decided it was time to leave for the grape harvest as it worked its way up north. On our last night, we said goodbye to Delphine and Genevieve. I had a wonderful night with her in a hotel, making love and discussing the possibility of seeing her in London later that year.

We were back on the road the next morning, thumbs out. We made it to Lyon in record time, walked to the outskirts, and stuck our thumbs out again. Alas, this time, we weren't as lucky. After not getting any ride offers all day, we decided to split up and go our own way.

Liam walked up the road, but I stayed put. I stuck out my thumb, and after a few minutes, a very attractive French woman in her early 30s pulled over. I asked her if she wouldn't mind picking up Liam. She asked me if I was sure that's what I really wanted. There was a seductive look in her eyes that told me to say no. We drove by Liam, and like so many others on my voyage; he slipped into my memory.

Chapter 16

Teaching English and Celeste

Her name was Celeste, and she was a single mother of a young eleven-year-old boy. She was a beautiful brunette with a great body and a very direct, liberated '70s attitude. In her best but broken English, she told me she would love it if I would come home with her to be her lover and teach English to her son, Louis.

I thought about it for a millisecond and told her I wasn't a teacher, but I could try tutoring him in spoken English. Celeste said that was what she was looking for, as he was learning grammar in school and she was teaching him grammar too, but she needed someone her son could practice his English.

What could I say? It was an offer I couldn't, and wouldn't, refuse. It sounded like an interesting adventure. She lived in a nice, small, older house on about two acres of land in a rural, wooded area outside Lyon.

Louis was a very inquisitive boy and was a quick learner. I'd talk to him throughout the day in English, and Celeste would talk to me in French, as I let her know I was trying to learn as well. It was a great trade-off, plus she was a skilled cook and lover. She had a huge sexual appetite, and we made love almost every day and night, which was fine with my young horny self.

I stayed for well over a month, but decided it was time to hit the road again. I could have stayed there forever with the two of them, but I was getting restless; the travel bug, once again, was itching to be scratched.

WILD CHILD

Neither Celeste nor Louis were thrilled about my decision, but I had to get back out there. Our last week comprised nightly parties celebrating our time together. Celeste loved to have sex outdoors, so every night that week, we spent under the stars.

The morning of my departure was difficult; both of them had tears running down their cheeks. By this time, I had become pretty good at saying goodbye (as I had to do it so often), but this one was particularly tough.

I ended up walking away backward, waving goodbye to them, but my chief concern was young Louis. It's hard to grow up without a father, and I'm sure Celeste was also aware of this fact. She was clearly looking for someone to partner with, and I must admit, it was very tempting. But I had already made my decision.

As I disappeared around the corner from their home, I stuck my thumb out and got busy trying to hitch a ride up north to catch up with the grape harvest.

Chapter 17

The Grape Harvest

It took me a few days to find the harvest, but eventually, I did, and I immediately got a job as a porter. The porter's job was to walk around with a large container on their back while the pickers dropped the grapes into it. I'd then take the grapes to the larger containers on the ground and drop them off there. It was better than bending over all day picking grapes, as I am over six feet tall, and it's a long way down to reach those lower grapes.

Most patrons on the wineries would feed you and offer you a bottle of wine a day. It was a great way to make a living. I found working there was similar to being on the kibbutz. There was a delightful mixture of young Europeans, Arabs, and travelers like myself working the grapes.

I made friends with a German guy named Johann, another porter. He also told me about running cars from Germany to the east. I came up with a travel plan. When I was done working the grapes, I made my way to Paris for a while, then to Zurich to see Renata. Then I'd head over to Munich to run a car to the east. After that, I'd decide what to do from there.

I followed the grape work to the Champagne region and then headed to Paris, where I only spent a couple of days. I figured I'd have plenty of opportunities to see Paris another time, so I hit the road again, eager to see Renata.

WILD CHILD

It was about seven hundred miles to Zurich, and it took me three days to arrive there, finally. As it was now early October, the weather was turning frigid. By the time I left France, my linguistic skills had vastly improved. I could communicate in basic French, so all my studying and practicing French had paid off.

Chapter 18

The Flaming Red Head

I arrived in Zurich in the early morning; believing that Renata would be at work, I spent the day walking around, familiarizing myself with the town again.

I bought a single, long-stem red rose and wrote a note saying I had arrived and that I'd meet her at 7:00 pm at her favorite pub. I leaned the rose next to the front door of her building. Renata's home was in Old Zurich; the streets were lined with cobblestones, and, better yet, no cars were allowed. It gave the city an old-world charm.

I waited in the pub, and right at 7:00 p.m., Renata entered with a big smile on her face. We hugged and kissed for the first five minutes and then ordered drinks.

Her friend Gertrude showed up. We had met previously that summer and got along very well. More of Renata's friends showed up, and soon we had a full table. We had a good time closing the pub down; afterward, we walked through the old town singing Neil Young's "Cinnamon Girl."

The next day, Friday was a workday for Renata, so I spent the day alternating between roaming the city and listening to albums in her apartment. She came home, and we cooked dinner together; my culinary skills left something to be desired, so Renata picked up the slack.

We returned to the pub later and hung out with the regulars. Renata asked me how long I would be staying, and I told her I wasn't sure, but probably for a month if that was okay with her. She smiled and kissed me.

She told me a big Halloween celebration was coming up soon; it was an event she went to every year. This year was different, though. She would make costumes for the two of us. That sounded like a blast since I enjoyed getting done up in costumes for Halloween.

I knew I should find a job since my French francs wouldn't last long in Switzerland, with the exchange rate being 4 to 1 favoring the Swiss franc. At that rate, I would run out of money fast.

I told Renata, but she said it would be hard for me to land a job as a non-resident in Switzerland. She told me Swiss businesses were fined harshly for hiring non-residents. I tried anyway only to discover she was right; every business owner I spoke to turned me down flat.

Frustrated, I told her that I might need to leave before the end of the month, depending on how long my funds held up. I knew I could make money by running cars out of Munich, so we would just have to make my money stretch out.

The time flew by, and my money stretched out just fine. Renata made our costumes, and we headed out that night to a series of parties. With Gertrude tagging along, we walked from party to party, having a blast, getting drunk, and singing songs until we arrived home.

I planned to leave on November 1st, so the next day was spent doing laundry and packing. Renata drove me to the outskirts of town and we said goodbye.

She asked if I would be coming back, and I told her I'd be returning around Christmas. She said that would be perfect since she was planning on spending Christmas at her friend's home in the Swiss Alps and that I could come, too. I thought that sounded wonderful.

Chapter 19

First Run East

I stuck out my thumb and began my latest trip to Munich, about 350 miles away. I figured it would take me a day or so to get there if the rides were good. The first ride took me to Kempton, a little more than halfway to my destination. So far, so good.

I waited at the on-ramp for about an hour when a large truck pulled over. I hopped in. The driver was a long-haired hippy like me, so it made the ride a lot easier. His name was Ulrich, and he was from Denmark. We had a great time listening to his music and talking all the way to Munich.

We pulled over at a little café for lunch, and he insisted on buying me lunch, explaining he had spent a lot of time hitchhiking back in the day and knew money was always an issue. I thanked him, and we had a delicious lunch of good German food.

Instead of dropping me off at the off-ramp, Ulrich drove me all the way to the front door of the youth hostel on the outskirts of Munich. We exchanged contact information, and I told him to visit me in California; then, we said our goodbyes. I grabbed a bunk in the hostel and immediately after that made my way over to the train station to find a ride east; by now, I direly needed money.

As I walked through the station, I saw a large group of Arab men at a table that looked to be the right people. I didn't have to ask them anything because they sized me up right away, asking me what I was looking for; I told them I was looking to drive east. The man who I was talking to smiled and offered me a seat.

A small man then approached me and introduced himself as Akbar. He was looking for a driver to Istanbul and wanted to leave in two days. He wanted to drive straight through in one haul. I told him that worked for me.

He asked about my driving experience, and I told him I grew up in Southern California driving on the freeways and had driven cross-country before. He was satisfied with that answer, so he stuck his hand out to shake on the deal.

I would make 500 German marks for the drive or around $250. Akbar told me that what we would be doing was illegal: smuggling cars into Turkey to be sold on the black market. My passport would have to be forged to remove the tax stamp to get out of the country. Most third-world countries have a luxury tax on all luxury items, including cars of 200% to 250%. They put a tax stamp on your passport when you come into the country with your car, and you either have to leave with the car or have a stamp that states you sold the vehicle and paid the taxes on it. Hence, the forgery. He wanted to know if I was okay with that. I didn't think too long or hard about it. I just shook his hand.

We planned on leaving the morning at 6:00 a.m.. in two days from an address he gave me. I went to an Indian restaurant that had been recommended to me, then headed back to the youth hostel to get some much-needed rest for the long journey that would take between twenty to twenty-four hours to drive.

Two mornings later, Akbar and I left promptly at 6 a.m.. for Turkey. We were each driving BMWs. Mine was a black, 1975 3-series hardtop, and it drove spectacularly on those winding, curvy roads across Europe.

I soon discovered that Akbar was in a real hurry to get to Istanbul. He had some setbacks with some of his cars in Munich and wanted to get to Istanbul to complete his deal and get back to Munich as soon as possible, as he had three more cars to deliver to Syria right after.

I followed him all the way. We drove straight through with stops for gas, food, and a few rest breaks. We got to Istanbul in twenty-two hours and went straight to a hotel.

He paid for the hotel and, after he sold the cars we drove in, would pay my fee. A couple of days of negotiations later, and the cars were sold. Akbar gave me my money and passport. I looked at my passport to see what the forgery looked like, and I couldn't even tell it had been forged. I thanked him, and he asked me if I wanted to drive another car with him to Syria. I said yes, so we agreed to meet back in Munich.

Before I left the hotel, Akbar asked me if I wanted to make some extra money on the trip back to Munich. He said all I needed to do was take a train ride, but it had to be in a particular compartment on the train. I asked him for more specifics because the hairs on the back of my neck were standing up; it sounded awfully fishy to me. He 'fessed up that the walls in the compartment would be lined with hash and that they needed someone to be in the car compartment the entire time.

I didn't hesitate. I told him, 'No, thanks.' However, if he still needed me to drive to Syria, I'd meet him back in Munich. He kept trying to talk me into it. A little too hard, I thought. I asked him why he didn't do it himself. It was only then that he gave up trying to hustle me. He said to meet him in Munich.

While I was in Istanbul this trip, I met an American, Ryan, who worked for the YMCA. He introduced me to many Turkish men who were merchants, artists, and actors. We hung out, smoked hash, drank beer, and talked about creativity in its many forms. We all became good friends, and whenever I was in Istanbul after that, I always looked them up.

Ryan also invited me on a trip he was planning in a year or two. We would travel the planet via the Equator by boat and on foot. It would be an outrageous adventure that would take a couple of years to complete, but it would bring us through some of the most amazing places on earth. Unfortunately, it never came to fruition; that was a shame because it sounded like a truly fantastic voyage, and I was looking forward to it.

Chapter 20

Steady Employment

I spent an extra couple of weeks in Istanbul and then hit the road again. To save money, I hitchhiked. I had no idea how good it would be, but just in case, I had the cash to take a bus if needed.

It was pretty cold as it was now mid-November, and I decided I needed to find a better jacket, which I bought from a friend in the Grand Bazaar. I made it back to Munich in three days time and went straight to the hostel. I was exhausted since getting a decent night's sleep is difficult while traveling in a car or truck. I slept peacefully through the night until the next morning.

When I awoke, I went to the dining room where I met a couple of Dutch guys named Lars and Sem. They were headed to India and points beyond. I told them about the car business, and they were interested. We hung out for a while playing music and then headed over to the station to talk with Akbar. Akbar was happy to see me, and even happier that I brought along Lars and Sem.

He spoke with them and verified that they could make the drive. When he was satisfied, he hired them on the spot. It worked out well for Akbar because he picked up a fourth car that afternoon, and he'd have enough drivers. We would leave for Damascus in a couple of days, but first, he needed to get the insurance papers together for each of us and the cars.

We left Akbar and headed to a pub that Lars knew. It had cheap beer and good food, my kind of place. We hung out drinking and playing darts all afternoon when three young ladies walked in.

Lars had a smooth tongue and no fear, so he walked right up to them before they even cleared the front door. As luck or fate would have it, they were also Dutch and from the same area as Lars and Sem. We all sat down and quickly paired off into couples. It was the '70s, and when it comes to the opposite sex, things happened quickly.

Their names were Eva, Mila, and Fleur. Fleur and I hit it off immediately. It was another fun night with new friends again, playing darts and drinking draft beer. We closed the pub down and headed into the night, feeling wonderful. Fleur and I detoured down an alley and found a semi-secluded area where we began to make out heavily. We ended up having sex in the alleyway up against a wall. After, I walked Fleur back to her hotel and headed for the hostel.

On the way back to my warm bed, I noticed three young, skinny Arabs coming out of an alley. They walked up to me and, in broken English, demanded that I give them my money and passport. Now, I was drunk but not that drunk. One of them reached out to grab me by the arm, but I knocked it away and hit him smack on the nose; he went down immediately. I took out my knife with its six-inch blade; I had been wearing it on my belt ever since being robbed in Avignon. The other two turned around and ran, leaving their friend on the ground.

He got up and looked at me. I put my knife away and asked him if he wanted to play. I knew he didn't understand me, but my actions communicated it unmistakably. He took a swing at me, which I blocked easily. He swung again, which I ducked. I countered with a left jab to his nose again and followed with a hard right to his jaw. He went down again. He was done, so I left him writhing on the ground and made my way back to my bed in short order.

I woke up early, feeling good about not having to roll over for those fuckers last night. I met up with Sem and Lars, and we repeated the day before, playing music and hanging out all day until the early evening when it was time to hit the pub again.

The girls had left for home that morning, so we were on our own for the night. That is, unless someone new came in. No such luck that night, so we drank and played darts, then went back to the hostel for a good night's sleep.

WILD CHILD

We awoke early and went to meet Akbar at the address he gave us, which was the same garage as last time. There were four newer Mercedes-Benzes parked and waiting for use; mine was a silver 1976 Mercedes 450SE, and the others were all newer 300D's.

We hit the road for Damascus right on time. Akbar loved to be punctual. It was about a day and a half drive. Akbar wasn't sure if we'd stop along the way or try to drive straight through. It would depend on the weather and our driving skills.

The weather wasn't bad, though it snowed most of the way. Fortunately, the heat inside my car kept me nice and warm. The scenery was breathtaking along the way, with the snow on the ground. Lars and Sem turned out to be excellent drivers, so we made it to Istanbul in about twenty-three hours, about the same amount as last time. Akbar decided to rest for the night there. We went to the same hotel, and we crashed until Akbar knocked on our door early in the morning.

We ate breakfast and continued our trip to Damascus. We had about half a day's driving left, provided there were no delays. But that was not to be. Soon after we crossed the Turkish border into Syria, Akbar was involved in an accident with a taxi. We were driving through the streets of Al-Safirah, a small town south of Aleppo. The damage was severe. The car's passenger front fender was bent into the tire so much that the car was not drivable.

A tow truck came and took the car to a body shop, where they bent out the fender enough so that it could be driven. Akbar said he'd get it fixed at his friend's body shop in Damascus when we arrived.

We hit the road again and, thankfully, made the rest of the journey without incident. We made it to Damascus in several hours. Now, Damascus is one of those ancient Middle Eastern cities dripping with history from every wall of the city.

Akbar put us up in a hotel near the center of the oldest part of town. We stayed for a few days while he sold the three cars that we drove. The three of us spent our days and nights walking around the city, seeing the sights, and tasting the local cuisine.

Akbar paid us our money, gave us our passports, and closed out our hotel room. I immediately checked out my passport and, to my relief, the forgery looked fine. He asked me if I wanted to make another run, and I told him I would. Akbar himself wouldn't have another run for a while, but his friends always had runs heading east.

Lars and Sem were now heading off to India on a very long bus trip. We said our goodbyes at the bus station and off they went. I was sure we'd meet again.

Chapter 21

Back to Munich Via Athens

I thought about returning to Iyala and the kibbutz since it was just a few hundred miles south to Jordan and the Allenby Bridge that crossed into Israel. But I needed more money, so I headed to Athens before heading back to Munich and another run east.

Being low on funds, I stuck out my thumb again. It was only 150 miles or so to Tarsus, where I'd catch the boat to Athens. It took longer than I expected, almost a full day; rides were short in the Arab world, except for truckers, who were usually going on longer trips.

I arrived in Tarsus after sunset, so I searched for a park to find somewhere to sleep. It took a couple of hours to find one, and by then, I was exhausted, so I went straight to sleep. It was cold that night, and I was grateful to have spent the extra money on a good goose-down sleeping bag.

I woke at sunrise and headed to the nearest open café. I bought some hot tea and tried a few Arab pastries. I settled on Swar As-sitt, which was a lot like baklava, but with an Arab twist on it. They were very sweet, so I could only handle a few of them. I lost a lot of weight during my trip, and my stomach had shrunk a good deal. You always lose weight when on the road because you don't eat that well or that often.

I headed for the harbor, and while it took a couple of hours to find it, I didn't mind, since I wasn't in a hurry. It was a beautiful day; the sun was out, but with a winter chill in the air. Plus, the architecture was gorgeous. Tarsus was founded over a thousand years ago, and it showed its age in its buildings.

I bought a ticket at the harbor, and as luck would have it, the boat was leaving in a couple of hours. I spent the time walking around the harbor, checking out the fishing boats and the larger vessels used for shipping containers. I've always loved harbors and the many different types of boats they have in them.

It reminded me of my earliest memories of my grandfather. He had a 55' wooden boat with twin diesel engines in Balboa Harbor in Southern California. I remembered my first visual memories of my life were cruising through the breakwaters at the mouth of Balboa Bay that led into the Pacific Ocean with my two older brothers, Bob, and Carey, and my older cousin, Chris, upon the deck, on the bow of the boat.

As I became lost in thought, the time flew by, and I thought I would miss the boat. I ran back and made it just in time. Since it was wintertime, there weren't too many people in the seating area. The boat was part passenger boat and part cargo ship, so I was lucky it was running this time of year.

Once we set out to sea for the three-and-a-half-day voyage to Athens via the port of Piraeus, I found a secluded bench and set up camp. The benches were wooden and hard on the backside, so I unrolled my sleeping bag to sit on.

I sat back for the long trip and pulled out my current book, "To Kill a Mockingbird" by Harper Lee. It's one of the all-time classics, a Pulitzer Prize winner made into a great movie, with Gregory Peck and Robert Duvall, one of my all-time favorite actors I wound up working with as an actor.

As the seas got rougher, people got sick. I managed to escape that seasick feeling; I don't know if it's because I'm lucky or because I never let that part of traveling by boat bother me. I kept reading and tried to sleep, which proved difficult on a boat that was bucking and rolling on violent seas. I was the only western traveler on the boat, so there wasn't anyone for me to talk with; most of the passengers were Arab and Greek families.

WILD CHILD

After nearly four days at sea, we landed at the port of Piraeus. The rough seas made it nearly impossible to make good time. I exited the boat and headed to the highway bus stand to catch a bus to Athens.

Once in Athens, I walked to Mary's Place Hotel. There weren't any private rooms, at least one I could afford, so I checked into a room with several beds; so, no privacy. I stored my backpack in my locker and headed out to get some good Greek food.

I needed money desperately, so I decided to sell my camera and lenses. I wasn't taking many pictures, and frankly, I was tired of lugging it around. I spoke to the owner of the hotel. His name was, oddly enough, Adonis, and he said he could help me out because I was a good repeat customer. I gave him my Canon 505 still camera with its two lenses (28mm and Zoom) to sell for me.

I headed out to eat and then grabbed a few beers to take back to the hotel. I ate at one of my favorite restaurants in Athens called Doris, which had great traditional food in a greasy spoon environment. I had a big plate full of Moussaka, a Greek salad, and a few beers for my meal. I know it sounds very touristy, but it's just damn good tasting food—comfort food but in an exotic setting. There's nothing better.

I bought a six-pack of beer and headed back to the hotel. When I walked into my room, it was full of travelers drinking beer and ouzo; I fit right in. I introduced myself to everybody, and we spent the night drinking, playing music, and talking.

I met a short, beautiful young Canuck girl from Montreal named Claudette. Her native language was French, so it gave me a chance to practice my meager French. Fortunately, she was willing to work with me on it, and I discovered she was as attracted to me as I was to her.

We got drunk and spent the night making love in the top bunk of a squeaky bunk bed. Fortunately, several other couples were doing the same, so it wasn't an issue. Claudette and I spent a few days together in a large group visiting the pubs and restaurants of the Plaka, having a great time.

One night, my bunkmates and I were sitting around in our room drinking and smoking hash when a conversation started about the Jonestown Massacre in Guyana, South America. It had just happened, and, like with any tragedy that involved a massive loss of life, it made international news. It was on everybody's mind. Jonestown was a small city in French Guyana where Jim Jones and his People's Temple had settled in an attempt to achieve some kind of racial paradise. Like a lot of noble intentions, things quickly went awry. Jones turned out to be a maniacal narcissist who oppressed his followers; when word leaked out about the horrible conditions in Jonestown, several family members of Jones' followers back home in America complained to their government.

Eventually, a team of concerned government employees, led by Congressman Leo Ryan, went to Jonestown to investigate the People's Temple. Jones had a couple of his more radical followers murder Ryan and a few others while they stood on the airstrip, waiting to board their flight home. This led Jones (while under the threat of being shot) to force-feed his followers kool-aid laced with strychnine. It was a horrible way to die and, to this day, in terms of human lives lost, is one of the worst tragedies in history.

My bunkmates were people from the Far East, the Middle East, Europe, Canada, and different parts of America. The folks from the Far East and the Middle Easterners were saying it could only happen in the West. The Europeans were saying it could only happen in America. And the Americans were saying it could only happen in California.

Everybody turned to look at me, so I said yes, but I blamed it on San Francisco, saying it could only happen there, which is where the People's Temple cult originated.

I told them I had four brothers who were all in a Christian cult in Arkansas that had begun in the country area near Los Angeles. They asked me if I had joined it, too. I said, no chance. I went there when I was fifteen and saw through the bullshit, so it skipped over me.

The next day, Adonis came up to me and handed me a wad of German marks for my camera. It was several hundred marks. I asked him if he made any money on the deal, and he said no, he didn't need any money. I tried to give him 100 marks, but he wouldn't take it. I thanked him and told him I'd be leaving for Munich soon but that I would be returning.

After a few days, it was time to head back north. I told Claudette, and she told me she needed to get to Frankfort to catch her plane back to Canada. We hit the road together, hitchhiking through the snow to Munich, with her continuing to Frankfurt.

We made a good couple. I was her bodyguard, and she got us rides. It reminded me a little of that film, "It Happened One Night," with Clark Gable and Claudette Colbert. In the movie, Gable, and Colbert ended up on the road and had to hitchhike. Gable fails miserably to get them a ride in a classic scene, but when Colbert hikes up her skirt and flashes a little leg, a car comes screeching to a halt. It was a little like that while traveling through Greece, except Greek men liked to play stick shift games with beautiful western women. A couple of men started their games, and I would lean forward and tell them to leave my girlfriend alone. One man pulled over and ordered us out of his car.

So, we got out and got a new ride in short order. Thank God for beautiful women. We got stuck in a blizzard at the Albanian border and had to sleep in the snow. No fun. But we kept each other warm all night; not much sleep, but what the hell. Once we hit Munich a few days later, we both went our separate ways.

Chapter 22

13 Mercedes and 1 English Ford

It was a bitterly cold mid-December day, 1978. An overcast and gray day with snow everywhere. My southern California blood was far too thin for these European winters.

I was twenty-three years old now, but felt much older. I had long blond hair and a full blond, red, and brown beard, and at 6'2" and about 195 pounds, I was pretty secure in myself that I could handle anything when the shit hit the fan.

I was sitting in the rear corner of the dining room of the Munich youth hostel, my customary back against the wall. I was reading "Steppenwolf" by Hermann Hesse for the second time; it was a complex read.

A young blond-haired guy, early 20s approached me. He stood there for a few moments, looking at me but saying nothing. Finally, he opened his mouth and, in a thick Australian accent, said, "What are you doing here, mate?" I laughed and said, "You know, I've heard that one before, mate."

He sat down, and, like so many other travelers I had met, we became fast friends. His name was Michael Grey, and he was a busker, which is someone who plays music on the streets across Europe to earn a living. He had just flown in from Adelaide, Australia, where he lived. I told him I had just come in that morning from Athens.

The next morning, I woke up late and made my way to the dining room, the central hangout for the travelers. Michael was already there at our corner table playing his guitar; I have to admit, he was pretty damn good at it. It was a full house with people from different walks of life with different degrees of traveling experience.

It was easy to tell the road people from the Euro Rail Pass trippers. Mainly the latter traveler's clothes were always fresh and clean, whereas road folks tended to be more ragged around the edges.

A couple of men walked in, and right away, I could tell they didn't belong, or at least I knew they weren't staying there. They were Muslim, and it seemed they were searching for someone. They made their way around the room, stopping to talk to anyone who would listen to them. My street senses went off. The hair on the back of my neck stood straight up, and I had learned through life experience to listen to my gut and my neck hairs.

They approached a young American couple, Euro Rail trippers, who were on a three-month blitz through Europe. I could hear their conversation. The taller of the two men was doing all the talking, and he was trying hard to convince them to drive his cars to Tehran. The Iranian city was falling apart at the time and not exactly a proper destination for this sweet American couple.

However, when I realized the American man was considering the offer, I felt compelled to do something. I got up, walked over to their table, and introduced myself. I told them I had run cars for some time now but to stay as far away from these two guys because they were obviously up to no good and had black hearts.

The couple didn't hesitate. They left in a hurry. I stood there smiling and staring into this guy's eyes to see if he wanted to do anything about it. Since he didn't make an immediate move, I returned to my corner table.

Thirty minutes later, after talking to everyone else in the room, they made their way over to my table. The quiet one just stood there, looking down at the ground, acting shy. The taller one stared daggers at me, then began speaking to Michael, making small talk. I was looking forward to this conversation.

I just kept my eyes glued to him; he'd look at me every thirty seconds. I could tell I was making him nervous. A few minutes transpired. Finally, he swung his head toward me and blurted out in a harsh voice, "What do you want from me?"

I told him, it's not what I want from you; it's what you want from us, and what are you doing talking to us. He looked at me with a badass attitude he found in himself. "You're not a good man." I laughed and replied, "I'm not the one trying to put people in harm's way like you are."

There was definitely a thick air of tension in the room. I decided to change strategies, go easy on the guy. I told him, "Let's start over, mate, okay? My name is Tracy, and I'm an American traveler." I extended my hand to him. He stared at it for a long time then shook it, saying his name was Ali, which is a very common name in his part of the world. It's like Joe or John to Americans.

I asked him what his deal was. He said he and his partners were taking fourteen cars to Tehran and were paying drivers 500 German marks to drive the cars, plus expenses. Five hundred marks were just over $250 at the exchange rate at that time.

I laughed and told him I just got paid 750 marks to drive to Istanbul, which was mostly true; I was paid 500. I countered that driving cars to Tehran, in the middle of the shit that was going on there at this time, an offer like his was way off the mark. I let him know that his lowball offer was an insult.

Instead, I said I'd do it for 1,500 marks, cash, with half paid at the Iranian border before entering the country. His eyes lit and he smiled. "You're very good, my friend." We went back and forth for a while until we agreed on 1,100 marks, cash.

Michael looked at me with concern. "I thought you said it's too dangerous of a trip?" I told him that for them it is, but for me, it sounded adventurous, and I'm all about that. I asked if he was going in with me. He thought about it for a minute before agreeing to accompany me.

So, I began one of the grand adventures of my life. We were going to be driving thirteen Mercedes and one English Ford from Munich to Tehran right in the middle of a third-world revolution that would topple that country's oppressive regime only to replace it with an even scarier one, one that especially hated Americans.

WILD CHILD

Years later, the Oscar-winning film "Argo" would tell a tale of Americans hiding out in Tehran during this time and of the rescue attempt that was conducted by the CIA. The great actor Alan Arkin said to Ben Affleck (who was in charge of the mission), "In Korea, we had suicide missions that had better odds. He wasn't lying.

Chapter 23

The Beginning of an Adventure

Over the next few days, we met the rest of the crew and the bosses. Ali was one of the latter. Then there was another man named Ali (or Ali 2 as I called him) who was a short, heavy-set Pakistani; he was always smiling, but it was a smile I didn't trust.

Then there was Ali's partner, the quiet one I met in Munich, named Muhammad. He was an Iranian and the brother of the main cat. He was the nicest of the four bosses, an honest, good man.

Finally, there was the big boss, Ahmed, also an Iranian, who would always fly home and back to wherever the hell we were. He was a very serious guy, the money man you had to go to for your handouts. He seemed to carry the weight of the world on his shoulders. He never smiled.

The crew was an assortment of nationalities. There was me, of course, a yank, who had already run cars a couple of times now, and Michael, the Aussie who had never done this before but was up for the adventure; that's the spirit I liked about him.

Michael also served another important function in our group as the resident musician. There was Pete, another yank. He was quite a character, a large gay man from Minnesota who wore sweaters too big even for his bulky frame. Pete was highly intelligent, an avid reader. We exchanged books all the time but never break the spine of one of Pete's books, or you'll never hear the end of it.

Next up were two Germans guys, Hans, and Frederick. They were on their way to India, so getting a ride to Tehran knocked off a fair amount of their trip. They were constantly smoking pot and always high.

The one female in our crew was a young English girl named Alice, with who Ali 2 had designs on and was constantly flirting with her. She was a little cherub of a girl, small, and round with the usual pale English skin.

Mark was a Canuck from eastern Canada. He was our sole fuck-up. He was often causing trouble by doing something stupid; sadly, the consequences of his stupidity usually landed in someone else's court, often mine.

Akram was our class clown. He claimed to be French, but we all knew he wasn't. Akram hung with the German boys, but only to scrounge their pot. He smoked but never had his own cigarettes, so he was always bumming them. Despite all this, I have to admit he was a fun guy to be around.

Our real Frenchmen were Jean Pierre and François from the south of France in the Mid-Pyrenees region. Very nice guys that kept to themselves, mostly. Their only problem was their love of heroin, which kept them stoned beyond comprehension. They were on their way to Bombay, India, to feed their habits. Bombay was known as one of the seedier underbellies of India and the capital of cheap heroin in the region.

Last but certainly not least was my new friend, Alon, from Israel via Switzerland. He was Israeli-born but raised in Switzerland; as a Swiss citizen, Alon had a Swiss passport that gave him more freedom to travel than an Israeli passport. He was fresh out of the Israeli Army and traveling the planet alone like me. He was a hulking, born Sabra. We would later meet up again in Israel after this adventure, and we became lifelong friends.

On December 12, 1978, our team set forth from Munich, Germany, to Tehran, Iran. You couldn't have come up with a better cast of characters to travel with on an adventure (or, for that matter, in a film) than this bunch that Ali rounded up for this trip. I was supposed to be back in Zurich to spend Christmas in the Swiss Alps with Renata, but I didn't make it back until early March.

What happened between that day of departure and the day I returned to Zurich was one of the most glorious adventures of my life.

Chapter 24

The Beginning of the Debacle

The next day, we moved camp to a seedy hotel on the outskirts of Munich. It was a real dump and a bad omen of what was to come. Pete was especially unhappy with our new digs; acting more like a diva, he figured it was beneath him.

We split up into two large rooms and slept on cots. Not exactly the most comfortable sleeping arrangements. It was Michael, Pete, Akram, Alon and myself in one room; while Jean-Pierre, Francois, Hans, Frederick, and Mark shared the other room. Alice ended up in Ali 2's room, which wasn't a coincidence. He was in hog heaven, smiling his crooked grin ear-to-ear.

We stayed in our room, and to pass the time, we drank a lot of beer and smoked even more pot. That helped us get to sleep, like a bunch of rocks, at 3:00 a.m..

A couple of hours later, I heard a loud noise outside our room. I raised my head to see what it was when the door burst open and several large German cops rushed into the room. They were waving flashlights and billy clubs in the air and yelling something at us. I didn't speak Deutsch, so I didn't understand what they were saying, but you didn't need to speak their language to understand what they meant.

They rousted all of us out of bed and kept shouting at us. I grabbed my passport and handed it to one officer. They forced us to our knees, handcuffed us, and put us against the wall. Michael, Pete, and especially Akram seemed pretty nervous about it all. Alon and I were taking it all in stride, waiting to see what happened next.

What was next was a false alarm. Apparently, we weren't the real criminals they were looking for, and as quickly as they had burst into the room, they cut us loose and exited.

Ali 2 burst into the room in a huff, accusing us of bringing the cops down on us. We stared at him then we all responded with a loud chorus of "Fuck off, Ali!" Then everybody but Ali 2 busted out laughing. He sulked out of the room, shaking his head and saying how we were all crazy. Nobody went back to sleep that night. We started drinking and smoking pot again and talking about our eventful night. We were pretty hyped up from it all.

The next day, we waited for Ahmed to get back from buying the insurance policies for the cars; one of the policy's guarantees was that the cars couldn't be sold in any of the countries we were traveling. There's a heavy 200% to 250% luxury tax imposed on each car sold legally in these countries, but our boys planned to sell them on the black market and skip the exorbitant tax payment.

A little lesson about traveling to foreign countries: when we entered each country, a stamp is put in our passports indicating you drove "Car X" into the country. You either need to leave the country with the vehicle or have a tax stamp showing that you sold it there and paid the 250% tax on the sale. Since our team of bosses wasn't doing either of those options, it created a minor problem.

But the bosses had a simple solution. They'd just forge our passports. Simple, right? It is if it's done right. But that's not so easy. It takes someone who knows what they're doing, and I didn't think these clowns did. I thought they're too cheap to pay a professional and would probably do it themselves.

You can use alcohol to rub lightly to remove a stamp; this practice is generally done slowly and carefully. If rushed and done half-assed, it leaves a smudge mark in the passport. But if they wrote any additional information in your passport with a ballpoint pen, the pen of the day creates indentations, and the ink stays in those groves.

The solution to this problem was to cut the passport's back cover, pull out the binder string, remove the offending page, and replace that particular numbered page and the binder string.

But that leaves a clear cut on the back of your passport, which sticks out like a black eye—a little scarier that way when crossing borders. In hindsight, we were taking an enormous risk for very little money.

The day was going by slowly and, while we were hanging out in front of the hotel, we decided to play a fun game I had just invented called "Breaking and Entering." Using a metal clothes hanger I had found on the sidewalk, we took turns trying to break into one of our cars, a Mercedes. Fashioning a wire coat hanger into a tool to open a locked car was nothing new. It was something I did all the time back home when I locked my keys in the car.

I should add that we played our game across the street from a large office building with a slew of windows facing us. We were in the middle of having a contest to see who could break into the car the quickest, when suddenly two VW vans came screeching up to us. The vans' door quickly opened, and out piled several of those massive German policemen, but this time with guns drawn, not billy clubs. We froze in our tracks. Akram quickly threw his hands above his head; this was nothing new for him. They made us all get down on our knees, put our hands behind our heads, and handcuffed us again.

Michael had walked away right before the cops arrived; he was down the street and started to come back, but I nodded him off. We needed someone left to let the bosses know we were in jail. And that's exactly where we were off to, once the paddy wagon arrived.

At the station, they took everybody's passports but mine. I had left it back at the hotel. They put everyone but me into one cell. I was put in a separate cell by myself, which I found interesting but somewhat unnerving.

It took several hours for the bosses to return from the insurance errand. They found Michael at the hotel, and he alerted them to our predicament. They then had to figure out which station we'd been taken to.

When they finally figured out where we were being incarcerated, they were not in a cheerful mood. It took nearly an hour of negotiations to get the bail paid and get everybody out of jail.

Everybody but me, that is. It seems the Germans thought I was the ringleader and held me on suspicion of being a member of the Red Brigade, a terrorist organization that was feared throughout Europe in the '70s. That got my attention!

That's the problem when you look like a leader or at least having a leader-type personality. It's great for an actor in casting, but not for a suspected criminal in Germany.

They held me for three days. During this time, I was questioned repeatedly. I finally convinced them I was just an American traveler who had done something stupid. They released me to the bosses on the third day with a stern warning about never returning to Munich, a request I later ignored.

Not surprisingly, the bosses were none too happy with me. My fiasco had caused a three-day delay in our departure time. I was catching up fast with the Canuck for this one. They couldn't just leave me in jail and get another driver since the insurance policy for my car was in my name; they had no choice but to wait for me.

Still, they chose me to be the lead driver. For another three hundred marks, I agreed. It meant everything the other drivers needed (including any complaints, arguments, requests, and such) went through me. I'd then relay it to the bosses. It kept them from having to deal with all the mishigas that might come from the drivers.

Chapter 25

On the Road Again

We departed early the next morning, a cold, gray day and snowing to boot. They assigned everybody a car but me. My car, a 1976 Mercedes 280S convertible, had broken down on their last trip. It had since been repaired and was waiting for us in western Yugoslavia.

It was snowing hard, making road visibility very difficult. Since I wouldn't be driving for now, I hopped in Michael's car for the beginning kilometers out of Munich. I would then alternate between Michael's and Alon's cars until we arrived in Yugoslavia.

The first leg of the trip was due south from Munich to Salzburg, Austria, a magically beautiful city. It looks like a city out of an old Disney movie. This particular trip could have been completed in two days, driving non-stop. Ours took a bit longer. Most of the Mercedes were 200D diesel, the staple of the taxi industries in Europe, the Middle East, and beyond. Akram got stuck with the English Ford, probably a good choice on the boss's part.

As soon as we got to the Austrian border, Jean-Pierre and Francois were suddenly afraid to drive through the border crossing. It turns out they had warrants for their arrest in Austria. They could have mentioned this little tidbit of information before, but I understood why they didn't.

I volunteered to bring the cars across. It sounded like a fun challenge trying to trick them. I drove Francois's car through, walked back across and hopped in Jean-Pierre's car, and drove back through without a hitch. Wash. Rinse. Repeat.

The tricky part was the guards had closed down the other gates. It was now riskier, getting caught with an Austrian stamp already in my passport. I pulled up to the same border guard as the first time. He looked at me sideways, but that was all. I declared nothing, so he opened my passport to the same page and stamped my passport. Luckily, they work by rote. Or they didn't care. Either way was fine by me.

As we entered Salzburg, Hans slid his car into a big snowbank, totaling it out. He had some bruises and cuts but nothing serious. The bosses drove off with the tow truck that towed the disabled car to a shop for repairs while we sat still, waiting for them to return.

When they returned, Hans hopped in with Frederick, and we were off once again. We left the banged-up car at the garage. There wasn't enough time to repair all the damage. We had to move on.

Chapter 26

Old Yugoslavia

We made it through the rest of Austria without incident and headed straight into Yugoslavia. We traveled on what I termed the Slaughter Highway. It's a straight two-lane road, one lane in each direction for miles and miles. Drivers are always passing slower traffic in very dangerous ways. It's insane what they do on the road there. The results and consequences of this driving are littered on the side of the road, namely wrecked cars all along the way. I think the authorities leave them there as a reminder to drive safely.

One of the Frenchmen, Francois, was sideswiped at 120 kilometers an hour by a car swerving out of the way of another car while passing. His car was number two that was totaled on the first day. Francois was okay, just shook up. His car, however, ended up on the side of the road, having spun out in the dirt and damaged from the other car's swiping.

Just like before, we waited for a tow truck to take the car away to a repair shop and then for the bosses to return. These accidents were burning time, making our trip much longer than we ever anticipated.

The next day, we made it to my ride, a beautiful and expensive Mercedes. It was medium blue with a light blue ragtop and chrome spiked wheels. It was also loaded up with two new TV sets in the back seat and a trunk full of booze, cigarettes, pornographic items, shampoo, and conditioner—all expensive and very hard items to get in these countries.

We started driving on the slick, snow-shaded road for a few hours; up ahead was a mountain range, not especially high in altitude, but treacherous all the same. The road became curvy as we snaked through the mountains, my car leading the way.

We came to a sharp turn, and I saw in my rear-view mirror that Michael had missed the turn and ended up in the dirt on the side of the road close to the cliff. I spun around, drove back, and parked. Everybody was standing around Michael's car.

I ran up and saw that one of Michael's front wheels was hanging over the cliff, and the other was right on the edge; the front part of the car was tilting downward a bit. Michael was still in the car, talking to Ali. I could tell he was scared and with good reason. His life was literally hanging by a thread... or tread.

Just then, Mark, the idiot Canuck, walked up and kicked the tire that was hanging over the edge. Ali pushed him back out of the way; everyone yelled at him. I shook my head and told him to please use his head. But this was typical Mark, always fucking up something.

Ali told Michael to start the car back up; it had stalled in the slide. He then told Michael to put it in reverse with the brake pedal still depressed. Michael did so; then, he began to press the gas pedal with the brake engaged. Slowly, he let his foot off the brake pedal, and the car started to move back. It then hopped off the cliff and drove back about 10 feet. We all applauded Michael, who had a huge but nervous smile on his face. If the car had landed another foot over the cliff, gravity would have taken over, and the car and Michael would've plunged to his death.

Chapter 27

Border Games

Yugoslavia is a very long drive. We'd been on the road for a while when suddenly we saw the Bulgarian border crossing ahead of us, and with it, another delicate dance was about to begin.

Unlike the Austrian border guards, these guards were no fools; they knew something was amiss when a bunch of twenty-something driving newer Mercedes pulled up to their border crossing. This meant it was time for *baksheesh,* for each of them in some form or another. *Baksheesh* is a bribe and a common way of life in that part of the world. No *baksheesh*, no business.

My job was to drive my car, loaded with goodies, up to the crossing gate first. Inside the car, I had bottles of Johnny Walker (Red and Black), cartons of Marlboros, pornographic playing cards, and magazines, and a few 8mm films.

I pulled up and gave the guard my passport. As he was going through his routine check, I pulled out a pack of pornographic playing cards and started looking at them in plain sight of the guard.

He was looking over real hard. I handed the cards to him and told him to keep them. I pulled out a pack of new Marlboros, opened them, and lit one up. This really got his attention because the cigarettes in Bulgaria are terrible and foreign ones are very expensive. I handed him the pack and said, keep them as a gift from me to him.

I was having fun with this, feeling like an old pro. The guard signaled me that he needed to check out the rest of the car and trunk; that was part of the plan. I opened the trunk to reveal a treasure chest of goodies: booze, cigarettes, and porn; the harder stuff. I handed him a bottle of Johnny Walker Red and a carton of cigarettes.

The other guards had taken notice by now and were coming around, effectively shutting the border crossing down. I began handing out all the inventory, then signaled for Ahmed and Ali 2 to drive up. They pulled up behind me and started talking to the guards.

The guards' boss came out of the building and approached us. That's when Ahmed pulled out the 8mm films, the golden ticket. He gave them to him and started negotiating for all the cars' passage forward. They made a cash deal, handed all the passports to him, and in half an hour, we were on our way again.

Chapter 28

Demolition Derby

We made it to Sofia, Bulgaria, late on a very foggy, moonless night. As we drove along the grand tree-lined boulevard in town, it looked and felt like a scene out of Doctor Zhivago. We drove slowly, taking it all in, but we were tired, having driven so many kilometers that day.

Suddenly, I saw Akram driving like a madman on my right, passing me at high speed. He lost control of the English Ford, and it flipped over side-to-side and slammed into a large tree, breaking the car nearly in half.

We figured Akram was dead, a gone pecan. We could see only smoke, fog, and wreckage. Then, as if in a dream sequence, out walked Akram with nary a scratch. He walked up to my car and asked if I had a cigarette for him. I looked at Michael, then back at Akram with wide eyes and open mouth. What could I say or do? I was dumbfounded and speechless. I just handed over the entire pack to him. The police came and arrested Akram. It turns out he was Turkish and a deserter from the army. So, he was shipped back to Turkey. I'd find out more later.

We found a hotel to crash in and slept like babies that night. The bosses decided we'd spend a couple of days there, as they had business to conduct in town.

Ali, Michael, Oded, and I went out to eat, then Ali took us to a Turkish-style spa. It looked ancient, as if it were built during the Roman or Alexander the Great era; it was that old. It had old stone walls that had seen much. There were large and small pools with different degrees of hotness. Conversely, the spa also had ice-cold pools.

Some large men gave massages the likes of which I'd never had before. My masseuse was whipping me with Birch branches to cleanse the skin and much more. I thought he was mad at me the way he was hitting me. When it was over, the beatings and massages left me feeling like jelly, but feeling great.

Chapter 29

Alexander's City

We relaxed and drank for two days, then hit the road early on day three, heading for Istanbul, a city I find fascinating. It's one of the most exotic cities I've ever been to, Constantinople (its former name), Alexander the Great's city.

I've spent a lot of time in Istanbul over my years on the road. I became friends with many of the city's artists, musicians, actors, and shop owners in the Grand Bazaar.

I did a lot of business there. I'd buy leather jackets and chillums, handmade, pileless rugs, and other items to take back to Europe to sell there. Then I'd buy 501 Levi's jeans, Kodak paper, and even sewing machine parts to sell to my friends in the bazaar. It was a wonderful time in my life, and I loved it.

Crossing into Turkey was pretty much the same as Bulgaria, but without the drama. The drive to Istanbul was uneventful, except for the act of driving my new car. It was fast and a blast to drive. I felt like a rich man. Pulling into Istanbul was a wonderful feeling. I felt like I was coming home.

Our hotel was on the Asian side of the city across the Bosporus narrows. It was a large cavernous building. Michael and I shared a room. The first place we headed to was Lyle's Pudding Shop. I often ran into people I knew there.

And as a bonus, there were plenty of beautiful European women. Michael, Alon, and I hung out there most of the day, drinking tea and talking to people who came in.

The next day, we headed to the Grand Bazaar to see old friends and show off my Mercedes. We met my friends there, including old Muhammad, the patriarch of a large family of merchants in the bazaar. Michael and Alon bought a few things for their families, and I bought three chillums to ship to my brothers; it was a splendid afternoon.

His family ran ten to twelve shops in the bazaar. It's an amazing place; centuries-old, steeped in history, with its open spaces mixed with small cubbyhole shops and larger shops lined with covered walkways.

I spent a lot of time here doing business and drinking chai with the merchants. There's a hierarchy to the system of those that work there. The youngest merchants are out on the walkways, selling gum and candies. The next level ones are selling chai on beautiful copper plates on the walkways. The teenagers and smart young ones are trying to get you to come into their shops. The young adults are working the front of the shops showing products and selling. And the older ones do the actual business.

And they all speak several languages since they grow up there listening to many languages their whole lives. That's where I lost my business virginity and learned how to negotiate.

Once I watched Muhammad sell a picture to an older American couple. It was a work of art to watch how he worked them and then sold them. You could tell two things about them as they approached. They were American, and they were wealthy. Being able to ascertain where people were from, and their income level, was a necessary art form needed in old Mohammad's line of business, and I learned it from him.

As they entered the shop, Muhammad gently engaged them in conversation and smoothly brought them into his lair. Right away, they said they weren't looking for anything to buy, to which Mohammad just smiled and offered them some hot chai and a seat on his pillows.

Once they sat down, it was all over, but they didn't know that. Muhammad knew if they sat there drinking long enough, they'd eventually see something they wanted; the shop was filled with many beautiful objects, all available for a price.

Muhammad introduced me as his young American friend with a Turkish heart. We made small talk, and I told them I was from southern California. They were from Connecticut and in town on business.

The husband told us that his wife always came with him on his foreign trips because they loved to go sightseeing. They were staying up at the Hilton on Taksim Square, an area I knew quite well. It was where all the expensive hotels were.

Whenever I was in town, I'd pay to stay in a flea-trap, fifty-cent-a-night flophouse with cockroaches, rats, and cold showers; but when I needed a hot shower, I'd go once a week to one of the more expensive hotels on Taksim Square to take a hot shower. I'd walk in the front door, but only if I could get by the concierge. If not, I'd go to the next hotel. I looked like a rich, long-haired yank traveling by backpack. I'd simply go door to door, from hotel to hotel, until I made a successful entry. Once inside, I'd look for an open room; when I found one, I'd quickly go inside and put the "Do Not Disturb" sign on the door. Then I'd take my precious hot shower and leave.

The wife kept looking at this one painting, whispering to her husband. He asked Muhammad about it; that was his moment to shine. Muhammad told the couple a great story about the piece of art. No doubt it was 100% fiction, but Muhammad was a master salesman. It was a sight to behold as he led them into the trap of falling in love with the painting.

The man eventually inquired about the price. Muhammad gave him the rich American inflated, tenfold asking price. The wife wanted it, and Muhammad and I knew this. When you play poker, you never want to give the other players a "tell" or signal what kind of hand you were holding. Here, the wife was showing us all of her cards.

The wife started to talk about money, but the man told his wife he would handle this, and then in a confident but pompous voice, he started to negotiate. At that point, Muhammad switched the tone of his voice and his body language, feigning defeat at the American man's superior negotiating skills.

The man got the price down a few hundred Turkish lira but offered to pay in dollars, something Muhammad already knew. He paid

Muhammad and then gave him a tip and a compliment. "You're a good man."

Muhammad had his son pull the painting off the wall to wrap up. He had made a few thousand American dollars for a painting and frame that probably cost him a few hundred Turkish lira. Muhammad was the genuine work of art. After they left, Muhammad's son put up another cheap painting on the wall similar to the last one; he threw some dust on it for good measure.

Michael, Alon, and I returned to our hotel. As we rounded the corner, we saw several police cars in the driveway of our hotel; we froze, wondering if we should continue. We saw Pete out front, so we went over to ask what was up.

It turns out our resident fuck-up Mark had gone down to Lyle's Pudding Shop to try to buy some hash. Of course, he talked to an undercover cop and got busted. Like the true idiot he was, he led them back to us at the hotel. The cops gathered up everybody's passports and put us all under house arrest. They searched our rooms. Fortunately, the French and German boys were good at hiding their stash. Otherwise, we would have been in real trouble had the Turkish cops found their drugs.

So now we were stuck in Istanbul. Everybody voted to kick Mark out of the group, but the bosses couldn't do that for the same reason they couldn't abandon me in Munich.

We kept ourselves entertained by listening to Michael's guitar playing and Frederick's harmonica styling. They were both individually talented, but together they were pretty damned impressive.

And of course, there were drinking games. The Aussies are well known for their drinking capabilities, and Michael was no slouch. They are also known for their drinking songs. We found ways to entertain ourselves.

Three weeks of house arrest later, we finally got our passports back. We prepared to leave as soon as Ahmed flew back into town. They didn't take Mark into custody, instead cutting him loose with a fine. He was damn lucky. As Turkish prisons are notoriously evil places on foreigners, especially westerners.

The next day, Ali 1 came to my room and asked if I wanted to go into town with him. I agreed, so we headed out into the city. He took me to meet his Turkish girlfriend, Alya, a very exotic, beautiful woman. We sat in the living room drinking chai and eating snacks when the door opened, and in walked one of the most beautiful women I had ever seen in my young life. It was Alya's first cousin, Aisha. I was in love. Or in lust, as my mother used to say.

We sat and talked for hours, and we returned there a few times over the next few days. We'd go out for walks or go to the movies, but always with Aisha's older sisters, as is their custom.

I went there alone one day. When I knocked on the door, I was greeted by all of Aisha's brothers and male cousins, all ten or twelve of them. They let me know in no uncertain terms that Aisha was off-limits to me, and it would be better for my health if I stayed on my own turf. I agreed, and as I walked away, dejected, Aisha looked at me through the front window. There was nothing she or I could do. I turned and walked away, never to return. I was heartbroken for a while, but instead of getting depressed, I drank it off with my friends.

On our last night in Istanbul, we went to a pub I knew. That night was rather uneventful, as there were no western women there. I had a good time anyway, other than still being heartbroken or lust broken over Aisha. I couldn't stop thinking about her.

Hans got drunk and started to get rowdy. His actions nearly got us ejected, but we stayed. I, too, got really drunk. We had to leave before midnight to catch the last bus back to the hotel; we should have left earlier in hindsight.

We left the bar and got lost finding the bus stop. Once we got our bearings straight, we ran and ran, making it there just as the bus started to leave. We ran harder to catch it, and fortunately, we did. The bus was full, as it was the last one to run for the night.

All the seats were taken by Turks, so we all stood in the back. Turkish bus drivers drive like they're racing go-karts on track, so it's always an adventure in keeping your balance; it's especially harder when you're drunk.

Many Turks emigrated to Germany for seasonal work, returning home in the off-season. The relationship between the Germans and Turks isn't very good, even worse than the one between Americans and Hispanic migrant workers back home.

Hans and Frederick started loudly talking in Deutsch about the Turks. I knew this because Alon spoke Deutsch and translated for Michael and me. I noticed that some of the Turks (those that understood Deutsch) were getting more and more pissed off and told them to shut the fuck up. As I said, there's a lot of bad blood there.

Soon, an argument broke out, and it quickly escalated to people standing up, ready to brawl, except it was the whole busload of Turks and only the nine of us. That didn't occur to Hans, nor did it deter him one bit as he jumped into the middle of them and started swinging. And then all hell broke loose.

One of the Turks threw a bottle and hit Pete on the forehead, cutting him pretty good. He had blood running down his face, but he stood right back up and got into it, hitting back at the Turks. Pete was a big man, and he was making his way through the crowd like butter.

I was throwing punches, too, and when I looked around, I saw all of us were in it. It gave me a weird sense of pride; I viewed it as a team-building exercise.

Some guy sucker-punched me from the side. I hate that. In retaliation, I broke his nose; it was hanging sideways on his face. I grabbed him by the scruff of his neck and his belt and used his head as a battering ram on the back doors. Having long since stopped, the driver responded by opening the back doors, which by now had shattered.

I threw the schmuck out the back door, and he landed in a heap on the sidewalk. Alon and Michael were deep into the fight, too, and I had to laugh as they were tag-teaming this big Turk with their blows.

The driver came around to the back and started pulling us off the bus. I started to leave but saw Hans in the middle of about four Turks, getting pummeled in the middle of the bus.

How the little guy had made it that far, I don't know. I fought my way up to him and received a black eye and a fat lip for my effort. I grabbed Hans from behind and started pulling him to safety at the back of the bus and then off it. He turned around and hit me on the cheek. I yelled at him, and he quickly came to the senses and smiled.

You see, I have this bad habit of rescuing people that can't take care of themselves. I guess in a former life, I was John Wayne, hopping on my big white steed, dressed all in white with my big, white ten-gallon hat, riding to the rescue with guns blazing. But rather than make me a rich and famous movie star, my habit instead often got me in deep shit.

We laughed all the way back to the hotel, but no one came out of our night unscathed. Pete got the worst of it, now having a significant gash on his forehead. Just the same, he was happier than a pig in shit. Back home, he would have gotten stitches, but we weren't home. We found a taxi stand and took two taxis back to the hotel.

Chapter 30

Back at It

Ahmed returned that night, and we headed out on the road the next morning, all of us hungover. We would travel through Ankara, the Turkish capital, and many small villages and towns through the mountains in Eastern Turkey, including Ezra, Jon, and Ezrican. We ended up stuck in a blizzard between those towns, close to the Iranian border with Turkey.

It was now the dead of winter, constantly snowing and freezingly cold. I wasn't particularly equipped for this weather, and neither were Alon nor Michael. Pete's car broke down just outside the village of Erzincan Havalimani, and we had to have it towed away, but this time it took most of the day, no doubt because of the inclement weather.

I remember this small village because Frederick left the keys in his car when he and Hans went into a little shop, and someone stole his car with all their stuff in it, including their grass, so they were really bummed. We were now down five cars, with nine cars remaining. We had thirteen drivers left, as Akram had been arrested in Sofia. All the non-driving drivers were now piling up in the remaining cars. Things were getting comfy fast.

We'd been on the road for five weeks now for a trip that should have been over in two (long) days. But I had to admit, it had turned into quite an adventure, and my wild child, black sheep personality, was loving it.

Our next victim was little Alice. She came to a turn in the road and forgot to turn, ending up in a ditch with a deep gash on her forehead; it would leave a nice-sized but permanent scar. I wasn't certain what caused her to crash, but she was probably putting on her makeup, something she did all day long. Her car was decommissioned, too. Down to eight cars now. This was turning into an auto-version of Agatha Christie's "Ten Little Indians." Alice ended up in Ali 2's car, much to his delight and her chagrin.

We were now closing in on the Iranian border. It was a nervous time. We all felt more than a little uneasy, but with good reason. Iran, especially its capital, Tehran, was coming apart at the seams.

The Shah was on his way out, and the country was erupting in violent protest. The leader of the revolutionary overthrow was Ayatollah Khameini, a religious zealot who was preaching from Paris, where he was living in exile. Iran was now a powder keg compared to six weeks ago when we started this little voyage.

But before we had to deal with that mess, we had arrived in Ezrican in the middle of one of the worst blizzards ever recorded in the northern hemisphere. And there we were, stuck at the bottom of a very large hill. We had no chains, so no one could get up the hill.

Finally, after a day and a half of being stuck there, I had had enough. After all, I'm a kid who grew up driving on the freeways of southern California, driving tractors as a child in North Carolina, in high school, and on the fish ponds at my kibbutz. Brimming with confidence, I jumped in my car, backed up, and then slowly gunned it. Much to my fellow drivers' shock, I precariously made it to the top of the hill and beyond.

But now, I was separated from everyone and stuck in a huge traffic jam that wasn't going anywhere. I was there for a few hours when I saw the others had followed suit and made it up to the jam. That night it snowed an unimaginable amount. The sub-freezing temperature took its toll on my car. It wouldn't start, and to make matters worse, the constant snowing buried my 280S up to the windows; that meant I couldn't get out.

As a bonus, I now had Alice in my car. She had gotten tired of Ali 2's stick-shift games. She was fine, but wore too much perfume. An odor my nose doesn't handle well. And in a small 280 S, it was like a bomb had gone off, further irritating my nostrils.

As if things weren't uncomfortable enough, Alice was a little smitten with me. Normally that would be great, but I was sick as hell from a cold, and she wasn't my type. But it was freezing, so a little oral sex turned out to be just what the doctor ordered. She was pretty good at it, too.

The sun rose early the following morning, and that was a relief. The high snowfall still had me blocked in, but luckily, I managed to start the car. I pushed the button for the electric window to go down, and I began digging my way out.

The snow was packed down overnight, so it was tough to dig out, but once I got out, I could walk on it. I helped Alice out and then saw there was a road crew station up ahead with a shed. We walked in, and to no one's surprise, it was crowded with everyone else stuck there.

The shed thinned out once the snowplows showed up and got busy on the road. I met up with the rest of the crew, and we assessed the damage. Two cars wouldn't start. I went back and discovered that mine wouldn't either.

Back at the shed, the door burst open, and in walked two obviously fucked-up westerners. Everybody turned to see them. It was a guy and a girl in their 20s; she was short but beautiful, and he resembled a tall, skinny weasel.

They walked up to Michael and asked him if he spoke French. Michael looked at them and said he didn't. The French guy asked (in heavily accented English) if we had any food. We laughed and said no. They then went around the room, asking for food from the truckers that were still there.

We later found out they were another couple of French junkies headed to India. Two truckers came up to us and asked if they were with us, and we said no. By this time, our new French friends were standing with us.

The truckers wanted to make a deal with our new friends. They would give them food if the woman fucked all the men still there; by my math, that was about eight men.

The couple were talking to each other in French. They were speaking animatedly, very fast, so I only understood bits of their conversation. It seemed the skinny weasel was in favor of it, but she was definitely not going for it. You didn't need to speak their language to understand that part.

By now, the truckers were growing more and more impatient, not to mention hornier and hornier. They kept talking to the weasel in broken English, letting him know they were set on taking charge and having their way with her, regardless of what she wanted. One trucker, a smaller guy, grabbed the girl by the arm and started dragging her off towards a side room where they were staying.

Alon and I looked at each other with looks on our faces that read, "Oh, shit!" We headed for the small guy that grabbed her. Alon grabbed him. The small guy hit Alon in the face, but it didn't faze Alon one bit. Instead, he grabbed the guy in a bear hug and squeezed. The guy was screaming in pain. Alon let go, and the guy crumbled to the ground.

I turned around, ready to go, waited for any of the other truckers to try something. Michael walked over to our side. Shortly after that, the rest of our western crew came over, too. It was now the seven of us against the eight of them.

The Frenchman stood on the sidelines along with the two Alis, Mohammad, and Ahmed. Nothing happened at first. It felt like a scene out of one of my favorite western films, "The Wild Bunch," when all the shooting stops and the heroes just look at each other and start to laugh. It was a standoff.

The girl was standing behind us, so they had to go through us to get to her. One by one, then two by two, truckers started walking back to the room where they had been waiting. The standoff was over.

After they left, the French girl turned and started screaming at her boyfriend. She went over and started slapping the shit out of him, then stormed out of the building. The Frenchman just stood there for a minute; he looked over at us then ran after her.

We broke out into laughter. Admittedly, it was a nervous laugh as we came very close to another gang fight, similar to the one on the bus. The French couple never returned, but we were still stuck there.

After the little dust-up, Ahmed talked to the mechanic and made a deal with him to start the cars. He wisely figured it was time for us to get the fuck out of there. But first, they had to get the cars out of the snow, which took some time to accomplish. My car started right up, but two others wouldn't.

Now we're down to six cars with eight cars left on the road. Ali 1 hopped in with Muhammad, and Alon got in with Michael, as my car was already full with Alice and goodies. We were on the road once more, closing in on the Iranian border.

We made it to the border in one push without further incident. The border crossing between Turkey and Iran was an ominous sight. One extensive building was painted half-red for Turkey and half-green for Iran.

We holed up in a hotel on the Turkish side of the border. Ahmed left for Tehran, and we waited for him. It would be a few days.

Then things started to get really interesting. Ali 1 and the Frenchmen disappeared, taking Jean-Pierre's car with them. My guess was they figured to sell it for themselves and split the money somehow. I thought, good luck to them. The car count was down to seven, with ten drivers left.

Alice hooked back up with Ali 2 in his hotel room. We saw little of them for the next couple of days. Then Ahmed returned, and we began to cross the border.

My deal, though, was to get half my money before we crossed the border. That's the deal I made with Ali 1, but since he had already crossed the border, Ali 2 was the only one there. I went to Ali 2's hotel room and spoke to him. He feigned ignorance, but I told him I didn't care; that was the deal I made with Ali 1, so no money, no crossing.

I told him, if need be, I would drive back to Istanbul and sell it myself. He said I wouldn't know where to sell it or to whom. I laughed and told him I'd run enough cars to Istanbul and had paid close attention to the players and knew exactly what to do and with whom to do it.

He started calling me names in Arabic. Strangely, most curse words in Arabic are about your mother or sister, not about the offending party. I blew up, grabbed his fat ass by the lapels of his pajamas, and pulled him out of bed.

WILD CHILD

I got right in his face and told him he had sixty seconds to fork over the money, or I was gone. Though he was scared of me harming him, he was even more frightened at the thought of me leaving with a 280S, so he got the money together quickly and gave it to me. I left immediately, heading to the border crossing.

Chapter 31

Do or Die at the Border

Michael and Alon were already waiting for me. We got in our cars, and off we went. The plan was I was to go last. Michael and Alon would go first, driving Michael's and Alon's cars. The others were waiting for us across the border.

I was waiting for Michael and Alon to clear before I went in. It took more than an hour because there was a long line of people crossing that afternoon. I saw them pass a window on their way to customs. It was my turn; I went and got in line.

Checking the scene out, I could see these guards were a no-nonsense bunch, but there was one man I didn't want to talk to in particular. He was in his mid-30s, tall, well built, with piercing black eyes. He seemed to be the head guy, and my gut instinct told me to avoid him.

When it was my turn, I walked up to the window and was glad that I was being waited on by a different man. He was a tall, heavy-set man with a mustache and wire-rimmed glasses.

Then out of the blue, the head guard walked up and relieved my guy; just my luck. He stared at me intensely. This was not a good sign. But I had to play it cool. "Good afternoon." He didn't take his eyes off me. He stuck his hand out for my passport, which I handed to him.

While I was standing there, Mark entered and walked up to an open window. I thought he had already crossed the border. This wasn't a good sign, either. I was beginning to think he was bad luck for me.

The head guard opened my passport and, in perfect English, said, "So you're an American traveler." My first thought was this dude, like many Iranians before him, went to university in the States; it was practically a custom back then. I nodded my head as calmly as I could. I was freaking out on the inside, but as was my custom, I looked cool on the outside.

He ran each page between his fingers, looking for waves from an alcohol wash. I couldn't help but smile. Not smart on my part. We were now in a duel with me as the prize. He held up my passport to the light, inspecting it for any wash marks or damage from them. I wasn't worried, since I had already inspected my passport for those very things. I did this as a precaution every time my passport was being forged.

Meanwhile, Mark the Moron got stamped, stepped back, and looked directly at me, smiling as if he had just won the lottery. *"I made it, Tracy!"* He walked away before I could punch him out. I turned and looked at my nemesis. Now he was the one smiling. He put my passport down, looked straight into my eyes.

"You will spend five years in an Iranian prison before you even see a judge if you live that long. Americans are not liked here very much, especially now." I didn't break eye contact with him. *"I'm sorry,"* I said with convincing naivete. "But I'm not sure what you're talking about."

"You're twenty-three years old and driving a newer Mercedes Benz, 280S convertible with two brand new TVs in the back seat. And who knows what's in the trunk, but I will know soon enough." He held his hand out. He wanted the keys, so I handed them over to him.

He went outside for five minutes. It seemed like five hours. When he came back in, he smelled like a cigarette. The bastard went outside and had a smoke while checking out my car. I sure as hell could've used one right then. My guess was he wanted to let me stew a bit (he was right). By now, I was more than a little concerned.

"So, you've got a trunk full of new stereo equipment, alcohol, cigarettes, pornographic materials, and washing products, the good brands only. And you look like a bum." He was right. I was looking more than a little ragged by then.

"And I noticed several of your friends just came through, all westerners. So, I figure you are the boss-man. Add five more years!"

"You know there's a revolution going on here, and you're an unpopular yank. Hell, you probably won't make it out of here alive or at least without prison."

With that, he stamped my passport but then got out the dreaded ballpoint pen and copied everything I had in my car across two pages. I was screwed. And judging from the big shit-eating grin on his face, he knew it, too. We were both taking this one personally.

When I finally got out of customs, I drove quickly to the meeting place. I got out of my car and walked straight up to a smiling Mark and punched him hard in the mouth, knocking him down flat on his ass. No one came to his defense. And not one person, save for Mark, was surprised at my actions. I just did what everyone else wanted to do.

Chapter 32

On to Tehran

We pushed through to Tehran without incident; well, almost. I was cruising along in my car, listening to Zeppelin on some 8-track tapes Pete had. It made the road trip less boring.

As I drove, I saw an apparition. On the side of the road, there was a pair of long legs connected to a beautiful, tall, red-haired woman. I love redheads, and this one had flaming red hair. And here she was, a woman alone, hitchhiking! In Iran! Half-naked!

She was dressed in short shorts, a tank top, and no bra. I pulled over and told her to get in. I asked her what the hell she thought she was doing hitchhiking in Iran dressed like that?! She said, in a beautiful Swedish accent, *"It's hot."*

She told me she and her boyfriend were driving to India and got into a huge fight, so she made him pull over to let her out of the car. She told him to fuck off. So, he took off and left her there on the side of the road. It was all over, and that she would get there on her own.

I asked her if she knew how the Iranian woman dressed there. She said, *"Yes, and it's criminal."* I said, *"Not to them. They are dressed head to toe in black with slits for their eyes because the Koran tells them to do so. It's a very religious country, and when in Rome, do as the Romans do."*

I said, *"You would need to change your clothes to something more suitable, and you're damn lucky you didn't get gang-raped by ten Iranians in a field somewhere."*

She said, *"You're right, thank you for informing me."* Then she changed right there in front of God and me. She took off her top, revealing her perfectly sized and shaped breasts, and then slid off her shorts. She wasn't wearing panties, either. And there wasn't a tan line to be found anywhere on that exquisite body; she looked like a model.

There I was, twenty-three, driving a fairly new 280S convertible Benz through the Iranian desert with the top down. Led Zeppelin was blasting on the sound system with an exotically beautiful, naked Swede next to me. I don't know what I had done right in my life up to this point, but by God, I was going to do a helluva lot more of it. Life couldn't get much better than at this exact moment with my twenty-three-year-old self. She put on some skin-tight jeans and a long-sleeved hippy shirt; she looked amazing. We talked like old friends all the way to Tehran.

Michael and Alon pulled up beside us and gave me a thumbs up, cracking up about my good fortune. I looked at them, raised my hands, and shrugged my shoulders as if to say, "What can a man do?"

Along the way, Mark got in a fender-bender at a stop sign. I guess they both thought they had the right of way. His car was pretty banged up, but still drivable. That made the score of six and a half cars that would make it to Tehran admittedly not a very good success rate. Ahmed wasn't too happy, and I didn't blame him.

We made two stops once we arrived near Tehran, the first in a residential neighborhood on the city's outskirts. It was Ahmed's home. The second stop was at a garage in town. We took turns piling into two cars for rides to our hotels.

Once we got to Tehran, I paid close attention to where we were going; I didn't trust our bosses any farther than I could throw them.

We were tired and worn out. Sigrid was asleep against my shoulder. I woke her up and introduced her to the guys. Ahmed wasn't happy that I had picked her up, probably because he had passed her up. But I didn't care about how he felt; I was happy she was with me.

It was 3:00 a.m.. by the time we arrived in Tehran. It took us over a month for a trip that should have lasted two days. On December 12, 1978, we left Munich and arrived in Tehran two days before the Shah's exit on January 16, 1979. Not good. The worst part was I missed my grand Christmas in the Swiss Alps with Renata.

But I wouldn't have changed a thing. I could've done without the heartbreak, but it was one hell of an adventure. In time, I would come to realize the real adventure was just beginning.

Chapter 33

Now it Really Starts

They split us up into two different hotels in the seedier part of downtown Tehran. Michael, Alon, Sigrid, and I were in one hotel while the others were in a hotel a few kilometers away.

Sigrid was given her own room, which turned out to be convenient for me. Ahmed wouldn't pay for her; it was against his beliefs. The hotel manager was against her staying in our room, so I sprang for it. That was when Sigrid pulled out a huge wad of German marks and said that she'd pay for her room.

I pulled her aside and told her she had a lot to learn about traveling the planet, especially alone. Rule number one is you never flash your money around. Rule number two is always to use a combination of traveler's checks and cash. We found the American Express office the next day and exchanged her German cash for some traveler's checks.

The hotel was full, but we were the only westerners. The rest of the hotel guests were short, dark, angry men, and their wives, dressed head to toe in their black hijabs. Everybody just stared at us. And the men stared at Sigrid, checking her out. So much for their beliefs.

All-day long, Tehran was under violent protests. The streets were teeming with poor Iranians flooding in from all over the countryside, and they were all angry and wanted the Shah's blood.

As westerners, we were always in danger of attack, especially me, the lone American. People would come up to me on the street asking, in perfect English, if I was an American. My response was to speak back to them in my own invented European Pig Latin that I hoped sounded vaguely Scandinavian or Germanic.

I thought I could pass as a citizen from Scandinavia or Germany with my long blond hair and reddish-blond full beard. But it never really fooled the Iranians.

One guy took a long look at me and said, *"Yeah, right, yank,"* and walked away. Whenever I went outside the hotel, my street hairs were always at full attention.

We felt it best to have safety in numbers, so the four of us stuck together as a group. Alon, Michael, Sigrid, and I became inseparable. We did just about everything together.

Our new hangout was a chai shop in the heart of the city. It was a large, cavernous wooden building. It looked like an old Wild West Saloon from the late1800's. It was filled with men of all ages and walks of life.

We sat down at an empty table. A few young guys struck up a conversation with us. Their names were Muhammad, of course, Amir, and Emir. They asked us what we were doing in Tehran. Alon explained that we were driving to India and got delayed. Otherwise, we'd have been out of here over a month ago. During our stay in Tehran, we would see these guys many other times in the same chai shop.

Drinking chai is an art. It is served on trays in shot glasses. You order several at a time. A bowl of sugar cubes comes with it. The locals will dip two or three sugar cubes in the Chai and then suck on them until they dissolve in their mouths. Then they'd drink the chai. I guess they enjoyed buzzing all day long on a sugar high.

Most of the citizens here also smoked hookahs and awful-smelling cigarettes. The chai shop was quite smoky. I skipped the sugar cubes and drank the chai straight. Alon liked the sugar cube technique. We'd spend hours there during our time in Tehran trying to maintain a low profile.

Later that day, we walked the streets to get a lay of the land. We saw many Iranians protesting and rioting. They were burning cars and thrashing businesses. We ended up near the government headquarters that were filled with office workers.

Suddenly, there were two large groups of protesters converging on us from both sides of the street. We were in front of a building that had a high wrought-iron fence surrounding it. Inside was a tank and many armed soldiers.

Michael and Sigrid started freaking out. Alon, being an experienced soldier who had fought in Israel, was calm. I was calm, but that's just my natural state of being.

As the groups got closer, I told the others, "I don't know about you guys, but if I'm going down, I'm taking several of these motherfuckers with me." I pulled out my six-inch knife that I had bought years ago for my Alaska trip.

We formed a small enclosed circle, all of us men back-to-back with Sigrid in the middle. I saw photographers taking pictures of this event, including us. We probably ended up on the front page of some international newspapers.

Several thousand people converged on us simultaneously from both sides. And then, much to our relief, people with flowers started reaching between the fence and placing them in the rifle barrels and the tank barrel.

They walked up to us, and we braced ourselves, ready for all hell to break loose. Instead, they asked if we were Americans because they loved America and their Shah. It turned out this was the first and only pro-Shah demonstration of the overthrow. We were obviously very relieved and talked with them for an hour and then left.

A reporter walked over and asked us some questions, such as "What the hell we were doing there?" We gave him the same answer we gave the guys back at the chai shop. We were traveling foreigners that unfortunately got delayed on our trip to India and got caught in the wrong place at the wrong time. We were, as Curly Howard once quipped, "A victim of circumstance."

As we were leaving, four young, beautiful Iranian women approached us. They spoke perfect English; that told me they had gone to university in America.

Normally that would be frowned upon for women in their country. It wasn't very common in those days. Most girls weren't allowed to get any further education after their primary education, if even that much.

The women invited us back to their house for dinner and drinks. Michael and Alon were very interested in their invitation. I looked to Sigrid to see what she thought about it; she was game, too, so off we went.

We walked for about fifteen minutes to where they were parked and got into two new Mercedes. No doubt these women were Shah supporters. We drove for about an hour to a very exclusive neighborhood and parked in front of a grand house surrounded by a high block wall.

We entered their gorgeously appointed home. The Shah's people did very well under him and his father. This home belonged to one of the women's parents who were off on a European vacation.

Of the four women, three of them were attracted to Alon and Michael; the fourth, whose house it was, was busy being our hostess.

We had a few drinks. Then Michael and Alon disappeared into the pool with the three women. The rest of us soon followed and found them skinny-dipping in the pool, having a fantastic time.

Sigrid and I went back inside and had dinner and drinks. Around midnight, Sigrid started to get sleepy. So I had our hostess order a taxi for us to get back to the hotel. Alon and Michael were nowhere to be found, so I said, let's go. Sigrid thought we should at least tell them we were leaving, but I told her they were big boys and will be perfectly fine here with their new girlfriends.

Eventually, Michael and Alon showed up back at the hotel a few days later, looking worn out but happy and no worse for wear.

Chapter 34

Riots in the Streets

The military was falling apart at the seams as more and more soldiers were deserting. Life was getting touchier out on the streets, so we stayed inside the hotel more often than not. We were able to keep up on what was happening not just by being there but through the *Washington Times*, a newspaper published in conjunction with the *New York Times* and the *Washington Post*. It is distributed across Europe and the Middle East. There was no internet back then, so every news item had to be read or seen on live television.

During our first two weeks there, Michael and I ventured out one morning and saw the streets overflowing with thousands of furious people. We could hear helicopters, their blades whipping the sky. We looked up and saw a large fleet of military gunship choppers flying just above the buildings. It was one of the last shows of military might before the military completely collapsed.

We walked for a while amongst the crowd until we saw a tank coming down the street with people all over the top of it. Apparently, the rioters had broken into one of the armories and confiscated the tank. Most of the rioters with the tank were strapped with American weapons.

It was starting to get a little dangerous, and Michael was beginning to get nervous. I thought it was amazing and exciting. I said to Michael, *"Don't you feel the adrenaline running through your body now? This is fantastic! Look at all this! You'll never experience something like this again in your life. Drink it in!"*

He just looked at me and said, *"You're crazy."*

We came to a large traffic circle near the telecommunications building. It was overcrowded with a few thousand rioters lighting cars on fire and breaking windows. Just then, two large vehicles entered the circle from different sides. They were water cannons with large barrels that shot water out at a powerful rate. They began shooting the cannons into the crowds, sending people tumbling down the street.

We were standing in the middle of the circle by now when I suddenly got knocked to the ground by a heavy hit in the middle of my back. I looked up, and a soldier was standing with his rifle. He had hit me with his rifle butt. He was trying to hit me again, but I reached up and grabbed the butt of his rifle, and pushed him back. I got up quickly, ready to have a go with him, when Michael grabbed me and pulled me into the crowd.

About fifty soldiers were pouring into the circle now. Michael kept pulling me, but I knocked his hand off me, thanked him, and told him I was fine now. I could feel blood running down the middle of my back from the rifle butt. I still have a scar in the middle of my back to this day.

We decided it was best if we headed back to the hotel and hibernated for a while. We lingered on the way back because there were too many people on the streets rioting.

We came to another intersection teeming with too many people. Just then, a car came zooming into the middle of the road, plowing into the crowd, sending people flying into the air.

One guy flew fifteen feet in the air and landed in a heap twenty feet from the car, obviously dead. The crowd converged on the car and pulled the driver out and beat him to death. It was time to get off the streets.

We made it back to the hotel without further incident. As we entered the lobby, I saw many people trying to get a room, and they were giving Michael and me dirty looks.

Michael immediately headed to our room. I followed, but the hotel owner, who was on the phone, waved me over and handed the receiver to me. I wondered who the hell would call me. Nobody outside of my little team here, Renata, and my mother even knew I was here. I said hello. A young woman whose voice I didn't know introduced herself as Nadia; she said she was the hotel owner's daughter.

She, her sisters, and mother had emigrated to America and were living in Rolling Hills, California, just a short drive from where I grew up in Orange.

She said her father was anxious about our safety in and out of his hotel. I told her so were we. She wanted to know what we were doing there in the middle of the Iranian revolution.

I told her part of the truth and explained our situation. She took a moment and said she was sorry, but that wasn't very smart. I laughed and agreed with her. We talked for another ten minutes, trading questions.

We hadn't heard from our bosses in some time, and we were growing concerned about that. According to Nadia, they had been paying our hotel bill regularly. One other issue that was even more worrying was we had not seen the rest of our crew.

That mystery was soon rectified. The next day, Pete, and Mark walked into our room. We were happy to see each other and went out to a store that sold beer. We found one that was still open, but it was in the seediest part of Tehran.

That night, we had quite a party. A little later, our German duo showed up. Naturally, we smoked a lot of pot, as our German boys, Frederick, and Hans, had quite a stash.

We had a fun time drinking, smoking, and talking shit all night. Sigrid got very drunk and fell asleep in my lap, so I helped her to her room and put her to bed. I went back to my room to continue the festivities.

The next morning, I went out to buy a pack of cigarettes from our local newspaper kiosk and found the price had gone up the equivalent of $2 a pack from the day before. I searched for a cheaper pack. It turns out prices for everything were going through the roof as the country's economy continued to come apart.

I bought several packs of Marlboro, as prices would surely be higher the next day. They tasted a little different here, so I suspected they were counterfeit or made outside the States. But they were still Marlboro.

It was early in the morning, so the streets were basically empty. As I walked around, I could finally see the destruction. It looked like a war zone with burned-out cars and trucks, broken store windows, looted and burned-out stores, and graffiti on the walls.

But I have to confess. Every single time I went out on the streets, I felt a sense of adventure and excitement. It dawned on me that I was, at heart, a bit of an adrenaline junkie.

When I saw journalists on the street, they would often want to talk. I had often thought about becoming a foreign journalist or photojournalist, but not because I had an overwhelming talent for writing. I just found myself drawn more and more to areas of strife.

Chapter 35

Ale, Ale, I Need More Ale

Alon and Sigrid had come down with the flu (or with flu-like symptoms), so Michael and I went out for some beers and entertainment that night. We searched the city for an open bar, but most were now closed because of the re-establishment of Islamic law and the imminent arrival of Ayatollah Khamenei.

We finally found one down in the red-light district. It was another cavernous Old West-style wooden building, the perfect environment for drinking beers. The beer of choice was Amstel, which I had grown accustomed to in my travels. The music was in Farsi, and while it wasn't quite the Rolling Stones, it was nice to listen to all the same.

There was an open table in the middle of the long, narrow space. As we walked to our seats, the room grew more and more silent; conversations stopped, and the men in the room stared at us.

We were used to it by now, so we just smiled and took our seats. Bit by bit, the noise level was raised as everyone resumed their conversations. I started to feel accepted.

A waiter finally approached us. He spoke only Farsi, the language of Iran. I had picked up a few phrases during my time there. During my travels, I had a knack for languages and picked them up quickly.

The waiter and I stumbled through a few phrases. I raised two fingers, said "Amstel," and rubbed my finger together, and improvised writing on the table. A real linguistics expert, right?

WILD CHILD

He wrote the cost of the beers on his order tablet. I don't remember the exact amount, but it basically told me that Michael and I had enough money to get properly pissed. A good night to be had.

The waiter left with our order. A few times during the night, Iranian men came over to our table to practice their broken English. It was always the same question: *"What the hell are you two doing here, especially now?"* By now, we had a set story that we came here on business and go stuck here and should be out of the country soon.

We had been drinking for several hours when we hit our financial peak. We were both sufficiently drunk by then, so I waved the waiter over and let him know we wanted two more beers and the bill. He got us the beers, wrote out our tab, handed it to me, and walked away.

I looked at the bill and froze. It was twice the amount he told us. Apparently, my sophomoric attempt at international communication wasn't too effective this round. I asked him the cost of two beers, but the waiter thought I was asking him the cost of one beer. I told Michael, and he started to freak out. I quickly calmed him down and told him to drink his beer. We would figure something out.

We had more money back at the hotel, but that wasn't doing us any good now. I don't think they would let us come back later (or worse, another day) to pay them; after all, we weren't exactly locals.

There was a bouncer at the door shorter than me but covered in tattoos and built like a tree trunk. He didn't look like the type that would be amenable to our situation. Nor did the rest of the crew there, both employees and guests, drinking on the eve of Khameini's homecoming.

I came up with a clever idea in my drunken mind to get out of our current dilemma. It sounded good to me anyway, though I wasn't sure how Michael would take it. I held off telling him until I finished my last beer. Michael kept looking at the front door, getting more nervous by the minute.

Once I finished my beer, I looked for a back door. I didn't see one. But in the intervening hours, we seemed to have faded into the background with our fellow bar patrons.

The bouncer was at his post near the front door. When I was satisfied, I leaned forward to let Michael share in my drunken brilliance. As I laid out my foolproof plan, his eyes just continued to grow larger and larger. He said nothing. I thought it was because he thought it was a brilliant plan. Well, I was wrong.

Michael looked at me and asked, *"Are you joking?"* I looked him dead in the eyes. *"No! Do you have a better idea?"* He shook his head no. I told him to relax. He took a few minutes and got up, saying nothing.

He started walking towards the door as if he was heading for the bathroom. As he got closer to the bouncer, he slowed down but kept going. Just as he passed the bouncer, Michael started running and made it out the front door. The bouncer turned to look at me, then started towards the door. I got up and started running with all I had.

Now, I've never been the fastest guy on the field, but I'm big and can get going and run over the right person if need be. The bouncer turned just as I was closing in on him. I dropped my shoulder and collided with him at chest level; it was like a fullback running through a safety. The impact sent him flying head over heels into the door jamb.

He was dazed and out, just long enough for me to get past him. Another guy stepped in front of me, but I gave him a forearm and shoved him down. I got out the door, headed straight for the rail at the street corner, and leaped over it like a professional track and field athlete. I took off running as fast as I could, pounding up the street after Michael, who was slowing down. He was weaving back and forth on the sidewalk.

I was catching up with him. As I closed in on him, I heard the 'ping, ping, ping' sound of a small-caliber gun being fired at us. The bullets were bouncing off the walls and sidewalk all around us.

Michael started to fall from running too fast and being worn out and drunk. I reached out with my right hand, grabbed him by the collars of his jacket, held him up, and kept running.

We soon came upon an alleyway, so I darted into it and kept running. I stopped to catch my breath and give Michael a chance to do the same. We came to a dead end with a large block wall covered in vines. Without having to say anything to Michael, he scaled the wall. I followed him. We dropped to the other side and fell to the ground.

As I gathered my bearings, I realized we were now in someone's backyard. An old man was outside in the middle of the night washing his Mercedes. I remember thinking that it seemed everyone drove a Mercedes in Tehran.

We got up and headed for the side yard and to the front gate, which led to a street. We jogged down the street for a while, carefully perusing each intersection. After enough time had passed, we started walking again, confident that we had lost our pursuers.

We got back to the hotel pretty late, and Michael headed straight to his room to go to sleep. I went to Sigrid's room to check on her. She was sitting up in bed, feeling much better. She invited me to stay and so I did. We were up all night having fun. I couldn't go to sleep because the adrenaline rush I was feeling was too great.

The next afternoon, Michael, Alon, Sigrid, and I walked back to the bar with enough money to pay our bill. Why? It was something Michael, and I wanted to do, though Michael was nervous about seeing the bouncer again. I told him if he acted nervous, he'll smell it on you and act on it. The bouncer was a street guy, and that's how they are. They act on animal instinct more than human logic.

As we crossed the street we had run down the night before, we saw a large group of men standing outside the bar. They were listening to music and speaking in loud terms.

By now, I realized they weren't arguing or even mad at each other; it just sounded that way. Arabic and Farsi are very guttural languages, and Iranians are very passionate people. Often, their talking may sound like an argument, but it's just them talking. Just like Israelis speaking Hebrew, it often sounded like they were fighting, but that's not the case.

As we got closer, some of the men recognized us from the night before and started walking toward us, including the bouncer, who looked like he had been through a meat grinder. His face and shoulders showed the markings of a fight, and his right arm was in a sling. He was wearing jeans and a tank top; it turned out he was quite muscular.

One man who approached us spoke pretty good English, albeit with a heavy Persian accent. He let me know that I had separated the bouncer's shoulder when I plowed him over. And after we had escaped, a huge fight had broken out in the bar.

Here's where the fun began. The bouncer walked up to the front of his crew and started screaming, tearing his tank top off. It was quite a sight and meant to intimidate us.

He walked up to me, and we played stare down. I didn't flinch. The bouncer nodded and moved on to Alon, who did the same as I had. He left Sigrid alone. Fortunately, by then, she had gotten the message and was dressing more conservatively.

He then looked down the line at Michael and immediately sensed his uneasiness and fear. He started dancing towards Michael by scooting his feet along little by little and pumping his fists in the air to imaginary music and singing James Brown's "I'm a Sex Machine." Needless to say, it was quite a sight to see and hear. As with many foreigners, they learn their English through music, TV, and movies.

Michael started reacting to the bouncer's wild display. He began backing up and stuttering. The bouncer just turned it up a notch. This went on for several minutes. Finally, I told Michael to stand his ground and to stare him down. Michael calmed himself down and followed my lead.

He looked directly into the bouncer's eyes. Instantly, the bouncer quit with his crazy antics and just stood there. Then he laughed loudly. Everybody followed suit, and we ended up having a good time.

We gave the money to the bouncer, who seemed pretty surprised by our gesture. We stayed for an hour and had a few beers before heading back to the hotel. Darkness was settling in.

Chapter 36

A New Escalation on the Streets

In the preceding days leading up to the Shah's overthrow, rioters, and looters had destroyed much of the city. Everywhere you looked, there were burned-out cars and stores, statues of the Shah and his father torn down, and anti-Shah and anti-American graffiti were abundant. Trash littered the city. It was a complete social breakdown. It looked like a war zone, and it was. It had been a tenuous and enthralling few weeks to witness. Then everything changed.

It was announced that Ayatollah Khameini would return on February 1. Suddenly, citizens went from destroying the city to cleaning it up. The route from the airport to where Khameini would stay was paid particular attention. Men and women were out everywhere cleaning the destruction with brooms, brushes, and, in some cases, even toothbrushes.

They were down on their hands and knees scrubbing the city clean. Removing burned-out cars and torn down statues; removing graffiti; boarding up broken windows, and much more. This went on day in, day out for several days and into the night, right up to the day Khameini returned.

I had never seen or heard anything like this, and it was very telling how dangerous these people were and would be in the future.

Chapter 37

Khameini Returns

February 1, 1979. Khamenei returns! The hotel was empty except for the four of us. They were all out on the streets, greeting Khamenei home after being exiled in Paris for fourteen years.

We decided this would be a good day to stay in the hotel, but I was itching to be out there in the middle of it. Everyone talked me out of it. We went out very early to grab food supplies for the day, but returned quickly.

We missed an eyewitness account of the festivities, but we watched it live on TV in the hotel lobby and outside our rooms on the balcony. It was quite a spectacle to see. The route from the airport to where Khameini would live was lined with hundreds of thousands of men and women; all dressed in black.

Chapter 38

Hunting Down the Boss

Our money was running out. We hung out at the hotel because we couldn't afford to do anything else. Michael, Alon, and I discussed our situation. We hadn't heard from the bosses since we arrived in Tehran. And that was over a few weeks ago.

We were in a tough situation. Sigrid said she had plenty of money to share with us, but we told her to keep it because she would need it for the rest of her travels.

We had a long conversation about what we needed to do. It was obvious our bosses had abandoned us, though they were still paying our hotel bill. We decided we needed to find them, force them to close our deal out, and pay us so we could get the fuck out of this mess, now known as Khameini's Tehran.

Luckily, I remembered a good deal of the route to Ahmed's house, where we left two cars and the garage where we left the others. Michael had some recollection of the routes as well, but since Alon and Sigrid were both asleep when we arrived in Tehran, Michael and I hit the road the next day to find these bastards.

We took off early in the morning. We had a map and very little money, enough to eat on for a day or two. We got lost trying to find the garage, but between the two of us, we could spot enough landmarks to find our way there.

Unfortunately, it was closed and locked up. There was a very tall wall with barbed wire on top, so climbing over was not in the cards. Even if we made it, what would we gain by being on the other side? We'd be trapped. We left and continued walking past the outskirts of the city.

Once out of the city, we hitchhiked, not knowing if anyone would pick us up. After about two and half hours, a small pickup truck swerved over to the side of the road and stopped, and the passenger door flew open.

We ran to the truck, piled in, and said thank you. He didn't speak English, and I only knew a few phrases in Farsi. We pointed to the location we were trying to get to on the map. He nodded his head yes and took off.

We drove for about an hour or so and came to a small city. I didn't recognize anything at this point. We came up to a traffic circle with a statue of the Shah's father. There were hundreds of people trying to tear it down. We were in the middle of it once again.

Traffic was completely stopped. So we said thank you and started to get out. The driver started yelling at us, shaking his head no, and sticking his palm out at us. We got the message quickly. He wanted money for the ride. It seems that there were no free rides in Iran. And they hated capitalistic Americans.

We gave him some German marks we had, and he seemed happy to get a foreign currency since the Iranian rial wasn't worth much at that time. We were happy to give him the money, since his yelling was attracting unwanted attention from the fringe of the crowd that was pulling down the statue.

We walked around the traffic circle, giving the crowd a wide birth. When we got to the other side, three men in the crowd started following us, so we started walking a little faster. They followed us for a good ten minutes, and we started to get nervous. Then, they turned down a side street, and we were relieved.

We walked for another fifteen minutes until we got to the outskirts of town again and stuck out our thumbs. After a couple of hours, a compact car pulled over with two men in the front. We got in and asked if they spoke English, which they didn't.

I showed the map location and asked how much money would it cost if we paid them in German marks. By now, I gave up using words and just showed them some bills and rubbed my fingers together, the international sign for how much money.

They showed us on the map where they were driving. I remembered Mohammad from the Grand Bazaar and negotiated with them until we reached a fairly reasonable price. They seemed happy but wanted the money up front. I shook my head no. Michael said just give it to them, but I didn't trust them. So, they took off without the money.

We drove for about an hour and a half when I started recognizing landmarks; so did Michael. The car stopped, I paid them, and we got out. We were now broke, and the sun was starting to go down, which meant it would get colder as it was winter now, and the days were getting shorter.

We looked at the map and tried to get our bearings when a brand-new Mercedes pulled over. Since we weren't hitchhiking, we wondered if he had pulled over for us or was just stopping on the side of the road. The car backed up to us; the window came down, revealing a man who spoke in a British accent, asking if we needed a ride.

We said yes and got in. He was a pro-Shah Iranian and told us the same thing all of them had, that he loved his Shah and America. He said he had been to America many times for business and travel with his family.

He asked us what we were doing in Iran and, more importantly, hitchhiking on the side of the road. Michael and I looked at each other and decided to tell him the truth… almost.

Michael told him our story. I filled in the blanks. We described the street and house and how there were many cars parked outside. He smiled and said he knew the exact house we were describing. I almost kissed him; I was so happy.

It turned out to be only about fifteen minutes from where he picked us up. When he pulled up to the house, we immediately recognized it.

We thanked him profusely, and he said to be careful with these people, that they were corrupt and evil. I told him we knew that about them. Though we offered this wonderful man money, he wouldn't take it. Kindness like his in a country in turmoil, like Iran, was as rare as finding a dodo bird.

The man drove off, and Michael and I stood there for ten minutes, discussing our plan. Plan? What plan? We really hadn't thought of one. I said, *"Let's keep it simple."*

We would walk up and knock and keep knocking until they opened the door. We walked up to the front door, and I knocked on it with authority. Not like a cop, just a solid knock. We heard nothing inside, so I knocked again. Then the door opened, and an older woman answered. I asked her if Ahmed was home, and suddenly, there he was in the doorway, staring daggers at us. The woman invited us into the house, a Persian sign of hospitality.

Ahmed, Michael, and I sat in a large room and started talking. His wife brought chai, followed by a full meal which we ate heartily, as we were starving by this point. After the meal was over, his wife removed all the dishes and disappeared.

We got down to business. We worked out a deal with Ahmed, something I didn't expect him to honor fully. The deal called for him to give us 300 German Marks to Michael, Alon and me and give us the balance of our money and fixed passports before the end of next week.

Ahmed agreed to the deal, which was a relief because it was getting very late. It was obvious he wanted us out of his house quickly. He gave us the cash and drove us back to the hotel right away.

Chapter 39

Just Killing Time

Upon our return, Sigrid, and Alon were happy to see us each for their own reasons. Alon was happy to get an influx of cash, and Sigrid was happy that we weren't killed out there; in retrospect, that was a distinct possibility.

The next week came and went with no sign of Ahmed, our money, or passports. We discussed returning to his house since we now knew our way back, but we thought better of it and chose to just wait it out for now.

We spent the next few weeks hanging out at the hotel. We'd roam about the city drinking chai at the chai shop during the day and drinking beers at the bar at night with our new rowdy friends.

One day we happened to be walking around the city and came upon an open-air bazaar that sold fruits and vegetables. It was located in a dead-end circle off of the main street. We browsed around buying fruits and talking to those who spoke English.

After we finished shopping, we found an alley off to the side of the bazaar and decided to walk down it. It turned out to be a fateful decision. At the mouth of the alley, I saw a familiar sight. Ali 2 and Alice were getting out of Mohammad's Mercedes. They were further down the alley, but this was no mirage. It was them… and I lost it.

I started shouting at them, then started walking at a faster pace towards them. People were stopping to look at me while the others tried to catch up to me.

I saw Ali 2 and Alice disappear through a gate. Inside the car, I could see Muhammad looking sheepishly at me. He was with another man I didn't know.

Michael, Alon, and Sigrid were trying to catch up with me, shouting for me to stop. But I wasn't having any of that. I launched myself onto the hood of the Mercedes and started kicking the windshield; it cracked like an egg. I leaped onto the top of the car and began jumping up and down on it as if it were a trampoline, denting it badly. I was yelling for fat Ali to come out and face me.

Of course, he wasn't about to come outside; he knew better than that. I paused for a moment and realized what the hell I was doing. I looked back up the alley at my crew and the Iranians behind them. They were all looking at me.

I started laughing about the little show I had put on. Then I started doing a little soft shoe dance on the top of the car, laughing all the while. Little by little, my crew started laughing at me, as did the Iranians. Everyone was having a friendly laugh at my expense; all of us except poor Muhammad, who was standing next to his car assessing the damage.

I jumped off the car just as my crew walked up and congratulated me on my dance routine. We heard Ali 2's voice from behind the gate, asking if it was safe for him to come out.

I told him he was safe from me, but I wasn't certain about anybody else he had ripped off. The gate opened, and out came Alice and Ali 2. Alice ran up to us and started hugging us. We were happy to see her. I pulled her aside and asked her if she was alright and if Ali 2 was taking care of her and treating her well. She said he was and that she would be staying there with Ali 2 for the time being.

Ali 2 and I looked at each other through steely eyes, as we didn't trust each other. Then I smiled at him, and he gave that smile of his, the one you just didn't trust. My feeling about him was that if his mouth was moving, he was lying. I walked up to him, and I could see a little fear in his eyes. I stuck my hand out to shake hands with him. He extended his hand, and we shook.

We stood there for a while talking when Alice invited us all into the house. It turns out they were living there. We went inside and stayed for a few hours, talking about our current situation and what we all were planning to do after getting out of there. We ate and drank and had a good time. Muhammad gave us a ride back to the hotel in his dented Mercedes. When we got there, we all went straight to sleep.

By this time, we were all frustrated with our situation. We had been in Tehran for five or six weeks now and were broke (again) and still no sign of Ahmed, our passports, or our money.

We went by Ali 2's house to see what we could find out. We made our way over there one morning; they were gone. They no longer lived there. Another frustrating sign. Now, what were we going to do?

We decided to pay another visit to Ahmed's house the next morning, but this meeting would be serious. We were going to hammer this out for good, once and for all.

That afternoon, we had visitors. Muhammad and Ali 2 stopped by the hotel to give us some money and told us we'd be able to leave Iran within the next week. This made us all smile.

There was just one problem. I was growing very concerned about my passport. The original border guard had written in mine, and I didn't think they would be able to wash out the pen mark and indents. That meant they'd have to replace the page. They would have to cut the back page of my passport on the inside, and if they didn't do a good job, it would stand out like a big pimple in the middle of your nose.

We spent the next few days anxious about our passports and how they looked after they were forged. I'd been through it a couple of times now, but Alon and Michael hadn't. I told them it wasn't an issue since their passports just needed a wash; no one had written in them, so they should be fine.

I also wasn't looking forward to saying goodbye to Sigrid. I had grown very attached to her, and she had likewise with me. She told me she'd fallen in love with me. She knew about my relationship with Iyala back in Israel and that once we were out of here, I'd be heading back to her on the kibbutz.

It would not be a pleasant moment that next week when I would have to put her on the bus to India. It was going to break my heart all over again. Hopefully, we'd stay in touch. I'm not into this attitude of 'Let's-just-be-friends' stuff; that's difficult but not impossible for me. But right now, I didn't want that.

Except now, I had no choice in the matter, as I was already deeply in love with Iyala. She and I had discussed what we were going to do as far as being with other people. While we were apart, we risked our relationship and open the door to being with other people. But there were no ifs, ands, or buts about it. I was going back to Iyala.

Chapter 40

Sodom and Gomorrah

One afternoon, the rest of the crew showed up at our hotel, ready to raise some hell. So were we. By now, everybody was very restless and going stir crazy. The monkey wrench in our party plan was that none of the stores were selling alcohol; Islamic Law had been established with Khameini's return, which was verboten.

We headed for our local bar, hoping it was still open. To our surprise (and relief), it was! We went inside and were greeted by our friends. We sat down to order some beers and drinks.

Some of my friends came over to join us, especially the younger ones. Soon we had a large group of partiers. We pulled together three tables and got busy.

Pete was flamboyantly gay, but when he drank, he'd turn up the gas on it. After a couple of quick shots, he let his freak flag fly. It was fun at first, but like with any loud drunk, soon it got old.

He started flirting with the younger Persians there, and some of them returned his advances. He grabbed two of them and started dancing with them, but that drew the attention of the rest of the bar.

I got up quickly and asked him to chill out. He refused until I got him to look around the room and see the looks he was getting. Pete was a very worldly and intelligent man, and so he got the point. He quickly sat back down.

We drank for a couple more hours when the younger men invited us back to their apartment to continue the party. Obviously, Pete was game, so the rest of us said, what the hell? The bar was closing soon, anyway. We bought some more beer, paid our bill, and left.

We walked through the night air for a short time and came upon a large apartment complex. We entered through the gate and then the front door. We took the elevator to the upper floor and exited.

The place wasn't very clean, but we didn't plan on staying too long. We entered their apartment, and it looked much nicer than the outside and hallway. They turned on some western music, and how great was that to hear after hearing only Farsi music for so long. A little Doors, Stones, and Zeppelin were good for the soul.

We started drinking more beers and smoking pot. The young men broke out some heroin to smoke; everyone passed on it except for Pete and Michael. Michael asked me what I thought, and I told him I gave that shit up a long time ago. He decided to try a little, but that turned out to be all he needed. He laid back on the couch with his eyes closed and took a nice, long nap.

Pete and the boys started dirty dancing. Quite a sight to behold. Soon they were all over each other, so I suggested they retire to a private room, which they did, slowly dancing down the hall.

We sat there for an hour, drinking, talking, and listening to good music. I looked over and noticed Sigrid was out like a light. She was a bit of a lightweight. Michael had come around by then, so Alon and I got up and went to retrieve Pete. It was time to call it a night.

We knocked on the door but got no answer, so we knocked again, a little louder. We heard a strange-sounding voice from inside saying, "Cooooommmmmeeee innnnn." Reluctantly, we did.

And there was Pete, in all his naked glory, in the middle of a den of inequity of his own making. His enormous body was intertwined with the three young men, and they were going at it whether we were there. Again, quite a sight to see.

They offered us some heroin and asked Michael if he wanted to join them. He said not a fucking chance. I told Pete he was the belle of the ball, but we were leaving, and did he want to come with us. He said he'd be fine, but thanks for checking in on him, and out of the room we went.

WILD CHILD

It felt good to be out of that mess. We woke up Sigrid, and the rest of us left, locking the door behind us. It didn't take long to get back to the hotel. At some point, Mark, Hans, and Frederick branched off from us and headed for their hotel. Sigrid wasn't feeling good, probably from smoking too much pot. I put her to bed and fell asleep next to her in my clothes.

Chapter 41

Preparing to Get the Hell Out of Dodge

When you spend a lot of time near people in intense times and situations, you form very deep bonds with each other. It's not unlike soldiers in a war. You're in that foxhole, each looking out for each other's back; you can't help but have a profound love for your mates.

Michael, Alon, Sigrid, and I had lived through such times together and had become very close. As our departure drew closer, a sadness was setting in. We knew we'd be going in separate directions, maybe never seeing each other again.

Sigrid was heading to India, though she was talking about heading back home. She would probably fly out since she had the money and could afford it. Michael's mom was an executive for British Airways, so he had a free fight out back to Germany, where he had a girlfriend that lived in the northern part of the country.

Alon was headed back to Israel via the route we had come, then south through Syria and the Allenby Bridge, and then back home to Israel. My route would be the same as Alon's, but I would run through Zurich first. I would be back in Israel several weeks later.

We would be leaving in the next couple of days, and as much as we all wanted to get out of this country filled with turbulence and turmoil, we didn't feel that great about leaving. I know that sounds strange, but we had mixed feelings about leaving; not the country, but each other's company. Mark and Pete showed up at our hotel with their passports and money. They were both quite happy and ready to party.

We wondered why the bosses hadn't shown up at our hotel to pay us off. I figured it would be a hard negotiation with Ahmed over my pay and passport, so I wasn't too surprised they didn't show up.

We headed back to the bar for some beers. We ended up staying a few hours before deciding to buy some beers and head over to Mark and Pete's hotel to drink there for a change.

We knew it was our last time there, and we were a little sad. We bought a case of beer and said goodbye to our friends at the bar, and left. It was about the same distance to their hotel as ours, but in the opposite direction. We stayed up all night drinking until the sun came up. We left drunk and happy, got back to the hotel, and crashed out in a heartbeat.

We were woken up early the next day, about mid-morning, by a loud knock at the door. It was Mohammad. He told us Ahmed wanted to meet us that afternoon at the circle near where Ali 2 and Alice had lived. I thought this was odd, but it put Ahmed on neutral territory and not on our home turf, so I understood. The game was on.

We waited until about 3:00 p.m., then headed over to meet Ahmed and Mohammad. Sigrid stayed at the hotel since she had no horse in this race. We got there on time, but they were nowhere to be found. However, there was a large mob there protesting… again. Another chess piece moved.

We waited about forty-five minutes. We saw Mohammad's Mercedes pull up to the curb at the entrance of the circle. We smoked a cigarette and then walked to the car.

Mohammad was driving, and Ahmed was sitting alone in the back seat. Alon opened the passenger side front door and got in. Michael went to open the back passenger door and started to get in, but I cut him off, since I wanted to sit next to Ahmed. I wanted to be in his face. I got in and scooted over next to Ahmed, and Michael got in behind me.

We sat there for a moment in silence. Not that long, but it felt like an eternity. Ahmed began talking to Alon, so he turned around to face Ahmed. He offered Alon the original 500 marks. Alon said that wasn't acceptable because what should have been a two-week trip took almost three months, and we're still in the country.

The day before, all of us had discussed what our deal would be. Alon and Ahmed went back and forth for several minutes. Alon was a good negotiator. They finally settled on 1,100 marks, a fair price considering the going rate.

Ahmed didn't want to set too high of a bar because he still had to deal with Michael and me, and he knew he would have to pay me much more, as I was his foreman on this long and winding escapade.

He paid Alon and gave him his passport. Alon asked me to check it. I thought the forgery looked pretty damn good and said so to Alon.

Ahmed then turned to Michael, saving me for last. Ahmed offered Michael the same 1,100 marks, and Michael said yes right away. No fun in that. I love to engage in negotiations as a participant or voyeur.

Ahmed then lit up a cigarette and sat quietly, smoking. I thought I could use one myself to calm my nerves, so I lit up. I loved this cat and mouse game we were playing. Ahmed finished his smoke, looked at me, and started talking. I held up my finger to tell him to hold on until I finished my smoke.

Now I smoke quickly, but I took my sweet time and savored this cig. It seemed to taste that much better. I flicked it out the window, turned to Ahmed, and raised my eyebrows to say, "Okay, I'm ready now." I could see this pissed him off, which made me smile inside.

He opened up the conversation, saying I hadn't fulfilled my duties as the lead man. I asked him how on earth he could come to that conclusion? He said it took too long to arrive in Tehran. I told him he was wrong; our delay into Tehran was due to the cars breaking down and the other drivers wrecking theirs. Mine was fine, as were Michael and Alon's cars.

I said the poor weather and house arrest in Istanbul were also contributing factors, neither of which were my doing. On the other hand, I pointed out that all the time in Iran was all his doing, not mine.

He sat quietly, nodded in agreement. But he was angry now, which only helped me, as negotiations should never get personal. But I loved how my moves were checking him.

I then threw him a curveball. I told him I wanted to see my passport now. I was concerned it was a bad forgery job. I felt he wouldn't want me to see it until after we had agreed upon a final price for my services.

He took a beat but couldn't deny me this request without showing me his cards. He handed me my passport, and I opened it to examine it. The first thing I saw was a huge cut mark on the back cover. It looked very sloppy and intentional. I was pissed but didn't show it. The rest of the passport looked fine; the new pages matched.

This gave me another negotiating ploy to add to my arsenal. But while I was checking out my passport, Ahmed pulled out a gun and was cleaning it with a handkerchief. It was a black 9mm pistol.

Oh, I thought, another new wrinkle, but what the fuck is this? I chose not to acknowledge it. Instead, I pulled out my six-inch knife and slipped it under my left arm so that it was close to his ribs. My thought was if he tried anything stupid, I'd be stupid first.

I told him I wanted 5,000 marks not just for making him a success but because of my passport, which could possibly end up landing me in prison.

He laughed and said all he needed to end this was to yell to the mob, protesting in the circle. He would say an American is trying to rob him, and they will tear you apart. He then raised his gun towards me. He smiled and told me the police would congratulate him for killing an American criminal.

Nice move, I thought. I paused for half a beat and checked out Alon and Michael. Alon was cool, but Michael was nervous, chewing on his fingers. I checked out Mohammad, who had his hand locked tightly on the steering wheel, looking at me in the rear-view mirror.

Ahmed and I stared at each other. I pushed my knife forward into Ahmed's ribs. He felt it and jumped back a bit, looking at me. I smiled and told him that before the mob tears me apart, I'll make sure they know you're a smuggler, stealing from the Iranian people.

And if the police come, I'll tell them about your car business and take them to your house and garage. He knew I knew where he lived and that he had cars there, but I don't think he figured on me remembering where the garage was. He had probably moved the cars from his house to the garage after we showed up on his doorstep.

It was a very tense moment. We kept staring at each other for what seemed like an eternity. Something or someone needed to break the tension. But I'd learned never to be the first to break, never cry 'uncle.'

Ahmed exhaled and shook his head; then, he smiled a little. So did I. Then the smile turned into a chuckle, and then he started laughing out loud. I did, too, followed by Alon, Michael, and even Mohammad. This surprised me since I figured things were going to get ugly. But fortunately, Ahmed flinched before I did. Game over.

He offered me 2,500 marks, and I shook my head no and came back with 4,500. We went back and forth, both of us enjoying the game. We ended up on 3,300 Marks. Middle Eastern men pride themselves on their negotiating skills, as do I.

After we concluded our business and payment, he said, "You American, you're good. You must be part Persian." We both had a good laugh over that one, and I got out of the car along with everybody else. We all shook hands and said goodbye.

Mohammad even looked a little sad to see us go. We headed back to the hotel to get Sigrid. We planned on making one more stop by our bar for one last night of partying before we left this bloody country for good in the next few days.

We got back to the hotel, which was still full of angry Iranians. I went to the office to talk to the owner. I learned that our bosses had paid the bill through the end of the week, so we were good there. I let him know we would be leaving in the next few days. That made him thrilled as he was always worried about our well-being.

Alon and Michael had already left for the room, and I started there myself. I wanted to tell Sigrid the good news. But then two Iranians stepped in my path to block me. I had had about enough of these people and was at my breaking point.

WILD CHILD

    I tried to walk between them, but they wouldn't budge. I clenched my fists and figured, okay, let's go, motherfuckers. Just then, the owner came running up, yelling at the Iranians in Farsi. They stepped aside to let me through. I turned and nodded thanks to the owner and went to Sigrid's room.

Chapter 42

Just Killing Time

Sigrid and I sat together and talked about our lives and dreams for hours. I told her I would always love her and that we would see each other again, but that I had to return to Israel.

She said Sweden is a beautiful country and asked me to come home with her now. I said I could never build something new without closing the door with Iyala, which I didn't think would ever happen. It was hard to say these things to her, but I couldn't lie to her and string her along. She cried again, and I just held her in my arms for a long time.

After a while, she seemed to be better. She smiled and kissed me on the cheek, thanking me for my honesty and tenderness. I asked her if she was up for one more party, and she said hell, yes. So we went to get Alon and Michael, and off we went.

We rounded up the rest of the crew at their hotel. Too late! Frederick and Hans had already left for India the day before. But Pete and Mark were good to go and saddled up with us for one last night of debauchery.

We got to the bar and discovered they had to close by the end of the week or face prison. I told them I was sorry to hear that, but the owner said it's a new life in Iran, and they had to play along. Of course, no one would ever have guessed the cultural, political, or religious changes that were coming to Iran.

We pushed a few tables together, and everybody sat down to drink. The music played, and Sigrid felt like dancing. So she pulled me out of my chair and began dancing a slow dance, no matter what beat was playing.

We must have been dancing for close to an hour when I felt a tap on my shoulder. It was Alon, and he wanted to cut in. Sigrid laughed and let go of me, and started dancing with Alon. They danced to a fast song, both of them laughing and giggling like children.

Everyone was having a great time. Then it was Michael's turn, and he and Sigrid danced for a while. Sigrid continued to drink and, being a lightweight; it didn't take long for her to get drunk.

Throughout the night, a few of our Iranian friends asked me if they could dance with her. I'd say sure, but it's really up to her. Sigrid kept up the dancing and drinking in equal measure and was stumbling. I gently guided her back to her seat next to mine at the table.

It was getting to be closing time. The owner walked up with a case of cold beer and said it was a gift for being such good customers. We thanked him, gathered ourselves up, and left.

Sigrid couldn't really walk. So I picked her up and carried her in my arms. But I couldn't make it all the way home, so we took turns carrying the lady of our crew.

We said our goodbyes to Pete and Mark, since we figured we wouldn't see them again, and headed for the hotel. Once there, I put Sigrid to bed and went back to my room. We stayed up well after sunrise, drinking our free beer.

Alon was going to leave later in the afternoon. He and Michael had already gotten their expired visas extended; that was something I would have to do as well.

I wasn't looking forward to going to the American embassy and handing them my poorly forged passport—no telling what they might do if they recognized the forgery.

I went back to Sigrid's room and crashed immediately. I woke up sometime later, feeling the greatest sensation. I thought it was a great sex dream, but it was Sigrid and she was frisky. We made love and slept and made love and slept all morning and into the afternoon. And it was beautiful.

A knock on the door awakened us. It was Alon, ready to leave. I invited him in since Sigrid was in the bathroom getting dressed. Michael soon followed, and we waited for Sigrid to finish so we could walk Alon down to the bus station. It was a sad walk. I was going to miss Alon.

When we got to the station, we said our goodbyes, and everyone gave Alon a big hug. I walked him to the door and told him I'd see him in Israel. We watched him drive away and then walked back to the hotel.

Michael would be was flying out the next morning, followed by Sigrid and then me. We sat around our room drinking, playing cards, and talking about Alon.

No one was in a good mood. We knew our great adventure was concluding. I knew mine hadn't ended yet because I still had to make it through the embassy and ten border crossings before getting back to Switzerland and Renata. We ate and went to bed early so we could take Michael to the airport early the next morning.

We got up just before 6 a.m., and I went to see if Michael was up. He was taking a shower, so I went back to my room and found Sigrid in the shower, too. I got in with her and we shared a wonderful shower together. I dried off and came out of the bathroom to find Michael sitting on the bed, smiling.

He asked if we had had a nice shower, and I laughed and said Sigrid needed help finding soap. Sigrid came out buck naked, and Michael's wide-eyed expression said it all. She had no body shame and was a very free spirit. Hell, it was the 70s. We got dressed and left.

We took a taxi to the airport since it was a long walk. We got there on time despite the heavy traffic. Westerners were crowding the streets of Tehran on their mad dash out of Dodge.

Most foreign businesses, embassies, and consulates were closed or closing down soon. The airport was packed. It had just opened back up to limited flights.

We ran to make Michael's flight and got there with just minutes to spare. We said a quick goodbye, and I told Michael I'd catch up with him in Germany later on.

WILD CHILD

He disappeared down the tunnel, and we turned and left. We took a taxi back to the hotel and then back to bed for a few hours. That night we chilled and stayed close together, talking and cuddling. Sigrid had decided to skip India for the time being and booked an early flight to Stockholm, close to her home.

The next morning, I sat in silence as Sigrid packed her bag. We made love one more time, and I told her I loved her. She cried again. Then we quietly got dressed and left for the airport.

When we arrived at the airport, we found out her flight had been delayed. We had about an hour and a half before her flight, so we checked her bag and walked around the airport holding hands. We ate and talked quietly.

They announced her flight was loading, and we both froze. I hugged and kissed her passionately. I told her I loved her, and we both cried. She leaned back, took her small hands, and wiped my tears away. She told me not to cry; we'll see each other again. I smiled, not sure if this was true or not.

They announced the last chance to board her flight, even announcing her name over the speaker system because she was late boarding. I walked her to the gate, and she disappeared down the ramp.

Back to just me again, the lone traveler. But that never lasted long because I always met interesting people on the road. That would lead to me hooking up with them and heading down the highway together, thumbs out.

I went straight to the embassy to face the music; either that or get my visa extended. I didn't know how I would fare. It took a long time to get there because the streets were very crowded, a mixture of the protesting mobs and westerners fleeing the city.

I got to the U.S. Embassy and saw a large crowd of protesters out front. I gingerly made my way through the crowd and came to the gate where the nervous-looking Lance Corporal told me they were closed. He said I should come early the next day if they were still here. All the Marines guarding the embassy looked very nervous about the crowd of protesters.

I went back to the hotel and hung out reading all day, something I loved to do while on the road but hadn't done since leaving on this adventure.

I woke up about 6 a.m., got ready, and left for the embassy. Once I arrived, the mob hadn't assembled yet, so I waited.

I showed my passport to a Marine Sargeant and asked him how long before the embassy opened. He told me they might not open today, but if they did, the time would be 8 a.m. It was about twenty minutes till so I just waited at the gate, hoping the crowd wouldn't show up by then.

When 8 a.m. they let me in, since the mob hadn't really gathered yet. I walked up to the window, handed the thin young man my passport, and smiled, telling him I needed to get my visa extended.

He told me I needed to go to the consulate and gave me a map to get there. It was only several minutes from the embassy, so I hoofed it over there quickly.

When I got to the consulate, it was open, but I was told they were closing the consulate down at the end of the day until further notice.

My thoughts were only that I needed to get my visa squared away today; otherwise, I had no idea how I'd get out of the country. I didn't want to attempt that without that visa stamp.

I thought about trying to skip the border crossings altogether and head north overland and sneak across the border. That wasn't something I wanted to do, but depending on what happened here today, I might not have a choice in the matter.

I handed him my passport, and he looked at it and looked back at me and said he'd be right back. Damn it, I wasn't paying attention, so I didn't see if he looked at the back of my passport or not. I was too distracted by my thoughts.

A different, more serious-looking man came out and asked me to follow him. Most of the rooms were empty except for the paper shredding room. They were working hard, shredding documents before their departure.

We entered a vacant room with several empty desks. In no uncertain terms, he told me to wait, since he was flicking my passport against his thigh quickly. I thought for sure the jig was up, that I was sunk; they had seen the cut. I wondered what they would do to me.

I waited for what seemed like an eternity. In reality, it was a very long forty-five minutes. He came back into the room, looking at me like I was a piece of shit.

He walked up and stood there for a while, as if he was deciding what to do or say to me. He finally handed me my passport and said good luck getting out of the country; then, he turned and left.

I quickly opened my passport and searched the pages for the visa stamp. There it was! They had seen the cut, I'm sure, but had chosen to try to help me out of my self-made mess. Hell, he was probably CIA and not a member of the consulate.

I looked at the cut to see if they had done something to it. It was untouched. Hell, they could have given me a new passport if they had wanted to, but I guess not.

I knew I needed to do something to mask over the cut, or I'd never make it through all those border crossings. I'd either end up in prison or have to pay out all my money in bribes. That included my emergency stash of five crisp $100 bills hidden in the frame of my backpack.

On the way back to the hotel, I hit upon what I thought was a pretty good idea. I'd tape my passport to hide the cut. That should work. I went to a pharmacy close to the hotel and bought a roll of light brown cloth medical tape.

I went back to the hotel and used it to tape up my passport cover. That way, it would hide the cut mark. When I was done, I thought it looked good. It looked as if I was trying to hide the fact that I was an American… I hoped.

At least they would have to unwrap the tape to find the cut mark, and most border crossing agents didn't have the time or inclination to do something like that… again, I hoped.

I was planning on getting a bus to Zurich the next day. There was one that left at 9 a.m. I didn't want to hitchhike this trip because I didn't think it was a wise choice, especially with what was going on. And with this passport, a bus was the cheapest transportation I could find. I could fly, but I was too cheap to do that. I hoped I would blend in with all the other westerners bolting out of the country in hordes.

I went to the lobby to say goodbye to the owner. The TV was blasting, and the crowd was cheering. I discovered that the embassy had been overrun by armed militia the day before, right after I left for the consulate.

Lucky timing for me, but not for the Marines or staff members. Some Iranians were killed and wounded in the skirmish, as were a few Marines wounded.

This was in mid-February 1979. Several months before Iranians took the hostages at the embassy in early November 1979. They were all lucky that day in February, as the Iranians only stayed for a few hours and then left at the behest of Khamenei's people. I said my goodbyes and went to bed.

Chapter 43

Back to the Border from Hell

The next morning, I left the hotel on foot and arrived at the bus station to find Pete already there, sitting in a chair, reading a book, something he always did. I was glad he was there because I had one of his books and wanted to return it to him. He was happy to get it back because he had forgotten all about it. Pete was headed to France so, we would travel together for some time.

The bus pulled up about 8:30 a.m. and loaded passengers. Pete and I grabbed the back seat bench after storing our bags underneath. The bus filled up quickly, and so did the bench seat, so we couldn't lay down to sleep. It would take us as far as Istanbul, where we would change buses to Strasburg in Austria. From there, we'd go our separate ways.

We settled into good books for our trip to the first border crossing, Iran, and Turkey, the toughest one. The bus was full of westerners from all over the world. I hoped my friend who had fucked me over the first time wouldn't be there; if he was, it probably meant I was dead meat.

I wanted to keep reading, but it was getting difficult to concentrate as my mind drifted to that border agent at the Iranian and Turkish border. If I managed to get through this first one, the worst thing they would probably do to me at any of the other borders was shake me down for some baksheesh.

I finally fell asleep but woke up halfway to the border. Pete was asleep, as were many others on the bus. I went back to sleep, woke up a couple of hours later, and started reading again; the rest had cleared my mind. It was an excellent book, "Mila 18" by Leon Uris, and it was an inspiring read, a real page-turner.

We started slowing down. We were getting close to the crossing. I woke Pete up so he'd have a clear head at the border. His passport looked good, even if it was still a forgery.

We waited for the border guard to come on the bus to give us instructions. He told us to come in groups of ten. That meant a long wait, plenty of time to stew or get calm since we were at the back of the bus.

Finally, it was our turn, and we got up to exit the bus. We were with a group of six Korean businessmen. We walked into the green part of the building and got in line. I began checking out the border guards behind the counter to see if I could see my nemesis. I didn't see him anywhere, which made me breathe easier.

Pete leaned in and said I looked a little nervous, which is odd because you're usually as cool as Cool Hand Luke. That made me smile because, as an actor, I loved that movie going back to the first time I saw it as a kid.

It also brought me back to my usual stoic self. I thanked Pete and waited. I looked up again, and I saw him! He was in an adjacent room, smoking and talking to a couple of other guards. His back was to me, but if he turned around, he would definitely see me. I started having second thoughts about cutting my hair and shaving my beard. But it was too late now to worry about that. Maybe next time.

I finally got up to the counter and handed my passport to the guard. He looked at my tape job and turned it around, and opened it without batting an eye. I passed the first test. He turned to look for the visa and stamped my passport. It had passed the second and most difficult test.

Just as I was turning away, my good friend turned and walked into the room. Our eyes crossed for a flash, and I swallowed hard. But he didn't recognize me, so I hurried to the next room and turned the corner so I wouldn't be in his line of sight.

The room was painted two-tone, half-green for Iran and half-red for Turkey. It was a waiting room for people coming and going to and from both countries. It seemed the Turkey side was moving faster than

WILD CHILD

the Iran side, which I found funny because it usually takes longer to enter a country than to exit one.

The crowd had thinned out, and Pete and I walked into the Turkish side along with the Koreans. One of the Koreans turned to me laughing, saying he had seen my passport.

He said, "What are you trying to do, hide the fact that you're an American?" Bingo, it worked. I just nodded, smiled, and said, "You caught me."

A guard walked up and took all the passports, which wasn't unusual, and he went back into a room. We stood there and waited. From inside the room, we heard Pete's name called out in a Turkish accent. Pete went into the room and came out smiling a few minutes later.

Then they called out two of the six Koreans. It took a little longer for them to come back out. They said something to their friends in Korean and headed for the bus. They then called in the other four Koreans, but not me. Damn it; this didn't bode well for my wallet, I thought.

They were in there for about twenty minutes. When they left, the one who had talked to me pointed to me and spoke to his friends in English talking about my passport, and they all laughed. I thought, I'm glad they're enjoying this because I'm not.

I heard my name and was glad to get to the next stage. The only real question was, how much was it going to cost me? If they found something, they could turn me back over to the Iranians. But my guess was they would pocket the money they got off people like me because they had families to feed.

As I entered the room, I saw a guard smiling at me with a 'Cat-that-ate-the Canary' look on his face. He was of normal height and weight, with the mandatory Arab mustache. I, of course, smiled back at him as he offered me a seat. He opened my passport and, after a few agonizing minutes, told me, "We have a problem here, good sir." Very polite this guy was.

I asked him, "How's that?"

"You don't have your vaccination certificate."

I smiled and said, "I'm an American; we get all that when we're very young."

He said, "But you don't have your vaccinations again," smiling all the time because he knew he held all the cards.

I said politely, "I've had them all, as do all Americans."

He then held my passport up to the light, looking at the separate pages and then directly at the back page.

"You don't have your vaccinations," again with a smile and no rancor.

I took the hint.

"Oh, you're right! Well, what can we do about that?"

His smile got a little bigger. *"You can buy a waiver from me."*

I prefer not to open negotiations, and border guards usually just tell you how much they want. I nodded and asked him how much that would cost, and, to my complete surprise, he said, *"Whatever you can donate."*

I thought, donate my ass. I bent down below the desk and took my right shoe off, which had 100 marks in it. My left shoe had much more. I separated the bills under the desk and offered him 50 marks, and he just smiled at me. I pulled the other 50 out, and he nodded ok.

He then stamped my passport, thanked me, and I was on my way again. I got back on the bus and made my way past all the unhappy faces; it had taken a long time.

I got to my seat, passed the giggling Koreans, and sat down. Pete told me he thought I was a goner. I said, so did I, for a minute or two. The diver closed the door, and off we went to Istanbul.

Chapter 44

I Love Istanbul

Turkey is a long narrow country, and Istanbul and the Iranian border are a long way apart, close to 1,100 miles. This would be a long drive on a slow, crowded bus and would take over two days to get there.

And truth be told, I hate traveling on buses and planes. You have no control, and I can't sit for a long time; I'm too active. Aside from a small walkway, you can't get up and walk around too much on buses and planes.

Every couple of hours, we'd stop for food and bathroom breaks, adding even more time to the trip. But these stops were a necessity for me. I needed any excuse to get out of this claustrophobic metal beast, so anytime I could go to the bathroom, stretch my legs, or get something to drink was a welcome relief. I have always drunk a lot, no matter if it's water, soda, or beer; I just consume a lot of fluids.

At the end of the second day, I noticed a Persian man sitting up front with his family. He was chatting up the bus driver over the last few hours. I was too far away to hear anything, not that I would understand it, anyway.

Not that it mattered to me. I was just killing time and satisfying my actor's curiosity. One trait I enjoy about being an actor is people-watching. You can steal little character traits for future roles by watching others. I continued to watch the action up front; it was the only game in town, or at least the only one I can see over the high seats. They started to argue, their hand gestures becoming more pronounced. It seems that all Middle Easterners talk with their hands.

Then the man started giving the driver money, but the driver didn't seem happy, so the man kept giving him more of it. It looked like dollars to me. I wondered what they were up to; I soon found out.

The driver pulled over and walked to the back of the bus. He signaled for us to get up. We didn't budge. Soon the man and his young son began walking to the back of the bus, and the driver got angry. He kept signaling for us on the back seat to get up.

The other people got up and walked towards the front of the bus, but Pete and I sat firm. Then the driver reached out and grabbed hold of Pete and tried to get him up.

I figured maybe we should get up, since the man was now yelling at us in Farsi. So we stood up, and the young son went and laid down to go to sleep. The driver was still waving and yelling at us but soon quit.

Unfortunately, we were barely beyond the halfway point, so we still had several hours to go. By my math, it was between 300 - 400 miles or five or six more hours to go.

Our options were now either to stand or sit on the floor. There were five of us in this predicament. I did both. I'd stand for a while, then sit for a while until my ass got sore from the hard floor, and then I'd stand back up again.

Like any other place I've been on the planet, the Middle East has its share of prejudice, discrimination, and racism. Since we were westerners, we were considered beneath them.

We finally made it to Istanbul around mid-day on the third day. As we were leaving the bus, I bumped into the bus driver and smiled, something I learned from my older brother Carey.

While we were getting our bags out, I accidentally stepped on a grocery bag that belonged to the man with the money. He wasn't too happy, but I was, even if it was an accident. I gave him a half-smile, shrugged my shoulders, and walked away a happy camper.

Like me, Pete was a very experienced traveler, so we both headed to the same 50-cent-a-night fleabag hotel. We had stayed there before.

WILD CHILD

Then we headed for Lyle's Pudding shop for some chai, cakes, and hopefully, some friendly, familiar faces.

The place was packed, and it took a while to get a table. From the Iranian border to Istanbul, the road we were on had been pretty damn crowded with all the people mass escaping from Tehran. And now it seemed they all wanted chai and cakes, too. Oddly enough, most people in there weren't road people, but business people and tourists.

Since Lyle's was mentioned in "Europe on Five Dollars a Day," everybody made a beeline for it now. Lyle liked the increase in business, but the rest of us could do without all the looky-loos.

One day while walking by myself through the grand open space surrounding the Blue Mosque, I heard a Turkish-accented English voice, *"Hey American, hey American."* I knew that voice.

I turned to see Akram walking up to me with a big smile on his face. His head was shaved for his stint in the Army. He looked funny, with his enormous eyes now more exposed.

We hugged and started talking, each of us catching up to the other. I was sure he was catching hell in the Army; he laughed and said true. But now, all he wanted was to serve out the rest of his duty, and then he planned to immigrate to France with his wife and children. I said, "What... you have a family?"

He smiled and nodded his head. We talked for a good two hours, or about the same time to smoke five or six cigarettes. We exchanged home addresses and phone numbers. We hugged again and said goodbye. It was very nice to see him again, and I couldn't wait to tell Pete.

On another day, I stopped by the Grand Bazaar to see Mohammad and his family. We talked and drank chai for a few hours; then I left, saying I'd see him next time.

We ended up staying in Istanbul for three days before we would be on another bus, this time to Strasburg.

Early the next morning, we arrived early at the bus station. The bus pulled up and, after we stored our bags underneath, we boarded and headed to the back seat. I was eager to get back to my book.

Chapter 45

One Last Time

I had to get across the border at the Turkish/Bulgarian line, and it was going to be financially difficult. Hopefully, that would be the only difficulty I'd face. It was only a few hundred miles to the Bulgarian border, and I surmised our arrival time in five or six hours.

My primary concern was my passport. I had already driven a couple of cars to Istanbul and Damascus, where they were sold, so now I had three forgeries on my passport. Up to now, no one had noticed them, but time would tell.

I spent the time finishing "Mila 18." What a wonderful book! I took a nap and was awakened by Pete when we hit the border. A guard boarded the bus and asked us to pass our passports to the front. He took them and left.

After a temporary delay, the guard boarded the bus and called on several people at a time to come with him to the office. That meant Pete, and I would be at the tail end of the line again. It was okay by me since I really wasn't looking forward to going through this again. In fact, I was worn out by it.

Soon, it was our turn, so we got up and headed inside. We waited in a loose grouping, in no particular order. One by one, they called people up. I had a sinking feeling that I'd be called last again, and so I was.

Everyone was already back on the bus when I walked up to the window and said hello. The border guard was a short, heavy man with a thin mustache and glasses. He didn't appear to have a sense of humor; he looked more like the by-the-book type, not exactly my type.

He held up my taped passport and asked me why I taped it up? I told him I had just come from Tehran, and Americans are in danger there. He thought for a minute, then pulled at the tape, all the while looking at me. I didn't flinch.

If he had asked me to take it off, I would've been screwed. Suddenly, a man who looked like his boss walked up and said something to my guy in Turkish. I looked outside while they talked to see what was up and saw that another bus had just pulled up.

I thought his boss was telling this guy to hurry things along. But I was wrong. He flicked at my passport and said, *"I see where you have come into Turkey many times this last year. Why?"* I remember thinking, damn, this guy is good and thorough.

I started to freak a little. I did not know what to say. And I was worn out by everything I'd been dealing with the last couple of months with passports and borders and cars and... women.

The light bulb came on then. *"I'm an American doing business in Europe, and I happen to love Istanbul, so I take short vacations and drive here with my girlfriends."*

He just raised his eyebrows. *"But you only stay for a few days and leave. Why? Where's your girlfriend now? And it doesn't show any cars on here."* He held up my passport. Damn, this guy was like a Turkish Columbo.

I completely crumbled and started babbling uncontrollably. I don't even remember what I said. I suddenly went blank and stopped talking altogether and stood there just staring at him.

Outside, my bus driver honked the horn a few times. The guard smiled at me like he had me by the balls, which he did. He said, *"This is going to cost you dearly. Have you ever seen the movie Midnight Express?"* I remember thinking, what the fuck?!

I completely fell apart at this point. He said, *"We don't like smugglers in our country. People like you, we lock up for life in a very harsh Turkish prison."*

I tried to ask him if there was anything we could work out shy of prison, but nothing came out of his mouth except squeaks. He laughed. I looked at him and started pleading with him.

Then, out of my peripheral vision, I saw a face emerge from the darkness. He walked forward and stood next to me. He spoke to me, but I couldn't quite hear him or understand his English in my current state of mind. I shook my head, trying to calm myself down. He was saying, *"Take it easy, my friend."* I thought I recognized his voice but couldn't remember from where.

He asked me if I had any money with me. I nodded yes. He said, *"Give it to me now."* I took off my left shoe and handed it to him. He looked at me as if I was crazy. At this juncture, I probably was. The bus driver came in and said he was leaving. The man from the dark spoke to him in Turkish and gave him some of my money. He returned to the bus and waited for me to wrap up my situation.

He then turned to the border guard, and they spoke for a few minutes with great passion. The boss man returned and talked to the border guard; then, he looked at my passport and joined in the conversation.

All the time, I wondered just how much more money this was going to cost me. Freedom really ain't free, especially at a border crossing with a forged passport. The dark man started giving the other guards a few bills of my money. When they kept arguing, he just gave them more of my money.

Finally, it ended! Everyone was smiling and happy… everyone except me. I thanked the guards, and, to this day, I'm not sure why. The dark man pulled me away and handed me what remained of my money. He said, "I'll see you back in Munich." So that was it! That was where I knew him from; he was one of the Pakistani men at the train station in Munich that runs cars east.

Chapter 46

Back on the Bloody Bus

I did not know how long I was in there. I clutched my remaining marks tightly and got back on the bus. As I walked down the long aisle to my seat, I caught a lot of dirty looks.

I sat down next to Pete, who took one long look at me and said, *"You look like you've seen a ghost."* Gee, was it that obvious from all the blood drained from my face or the money drained from my shoe?

"You were in there for half an hour." I was surprised it was that long. Pete asked what happened, so I told him. When I finished, he looked at me with big eyes and then burst out laughing. *"Cool Hand Luke, man. You are Luke! You broke down just like Luke!"*

I just stared at the floor, but once it registered, I started laughing, too. Once I started, I couldn't stop. It felt good to let it out of me; I needed that. I looked up to see everyone on the bus now staring at us.

I looked at my hand to see what the damage was to my war chest. I had 50 marks left. Then it hit me. I was supposed to take off my right shoe like I did last time. That shoe had 100 marks. But the left shoe had 500 marks! This escape plan was expensive, but obviously better than the alternative.

I sat back for a moment to rest my eyes and woke up sometime later in Sofia. I needed that sleep. We stopped to use the bathroom and eat. It was still very cold then, and I felt it in my bones. We spent a half-hour there. I grabbed a sandwich and ate it in a flash. Apparently, the threat of spending time in a Turkish prison gave me quite the appetite.

We loaded back up and left for the Yugoslavian border; that should be little to no problem for me. In fact, based on my experience, I felt the rest of the border crossings should hold little to no danger for me. But you never know. It would take several hours to get to the border, so time again for some much-needed sleep.

We arrived at the border in the middle of the night, and I'm sure everyone was asleep. The bus driver turned on the dome lights and walked through the bus, waking everyone up.

I woke with a severe headache, so I went up front to talk to the bus driver after making his way back to his seat. After a few minutes, he opened the storage bin. I found my backpack and my aspirin inside and took three.

And again, as if we were all in "Groundhog Day," the guards boarded the bus and collected everyone's passports. But this time, they called us in groups of ten, so the process went by faster.

When it came to be my turn, I started to feel nervous. I walked up to the window and gave the guard my passport. He held it up and laughed.

I thought, *Oh shit*. But he was laughing for the very reason I wanted all the passport busybodies to laugh. He thought I was disguising the fact that I was an American. He stamped my passport, and off I went.

I was thinking about Renata. I hadn't seen her since last fall when I left Zurich. I sent her a postcard letting her know I was out of Tehran and would be back with her in two weeks.

By this time, though, I wasn't sure she'd even want to see me. I remembered I had some of my belongings still there if she hadn't thrown them away. Come to think of it; I had bits and pieces of my stuff all over Europe and the Middle East.

We left our relationship on good terms. I'd written to her a few times, but my mail hadn't caught up with me yet, so I didn't know if she wrote to me as well. Either way, I'd find out shortly.

WILD CHILD

I played an ongoing game with the mail service. I had my mail sent to post offices in different cities. I would then have it forwarded all over Europe and the Middle East, trying to make it catch up with me.

Because I never really knew how long I'd be in any one place, the mail would eventually catch up to me, or I would catch up to it. When it did, I'd throw a little mail opening party since I could sometimes have up to six months of mail to read and respond. I didn't mind because I usually had the time.

The trek along slaughter highway was very uneventful this time as the bus driver was in no hurry. It's a long drive through what used to be old Yugoslavia, and it passes some beautiful countryside.

A few days later, we arrived at the Austrian border. It was a moonlit night with clear skies; the moon was high, and there were lots of stars. I was sore from the bus bouncing and rolling along the highway; it wasn't the best road back then, not to mention the bus was old, and the suspension had seen better days.

We got off the bus and lined up at the border crossing windows. I had no fear this time; after all, I was now back in the west. But then I thought, don't get cocky, Tracy. I walked up to and away from the window in less than a minute. That was a pleasant change of pace from the other crossings.

Since Austria is a much smaller country than the ones I'd been traveling through, the Strasburg trip took less than three hours. Strasberg is a majestic city with beautiful countryside that reminded me of Switzerland. The Zurich trip was also only a drive of a few hours. I thought about hitchhiking but thought better of it; the weather was freezing cold.

It was the middle of the night when we arrived. Pete and I found the youth hostel, got a bed, and crashed until late the next morning.

When I woke up, Pete was gone. He left a note that said, *"Luke, nice meeting you and knowing you. Maybe we will bump into each other again out on the road."*

Nice sentiments. I especially liked the "Luke" part. I loved the movie and Newman in it; in fact, I loved everything he did. I always thought of my father when I thought of Paul Newman. They were born and died in the same years.

Having made it through this journey without spending all my money, or worse, getting thrown into prison, was a gift. I was in no hurry. I strolled around Strasberg. I'd driven through it many times, but I had never really experienced it. I spent a few days eating, drinking, and simply walking around.

I met a couple of Aussies in a pub, and we got to shooting the shit and drinking some beers. I always felt good around Aussies. They are a fun crowd, wonderful mates.

The ones I met were headed back home over land since they had originally flown from Australia to London.

They asked me about Iran, and I told them the truth, strongly suggesting they take a flight over Iran. They were happy with my advice and said, *"Thanks, mate, we will."*

I said, *"Good night and good luck,"* and went back to the youth hostel where I fell fast asleep, which was not a normal function for me.

After a few more mornings, I decided I had seen enough of Strasberg. It was time to see Renata. I had a small breakfast and headed to the bus station. I waited for about two hours for the bus to Zurich to arrive.

Fortunately, this was the west, and the buses were top notch. I called Renata before buying my ticket. She was happy to hear my voice and said she would be waiting for me at the bus station when I arrived. Wonderful!

The bus took about three hours, so I spent the time drinking in the beautiful scenery. We pulled into the nice, spotless Zurich bus station after going through the border crossing in a flash. Again, no problems.

My flaming, red-headed Renata was indeed there, waiting for me. She ran up and threw herself at me, and I caught her in my arms. We had a big, wet kiss, and then we just held each other. An older couple walked by and shook their heads in disapproval.

Chapter 47

Where to Go Now?

It's now March 3, 1979. On December 12, 1978, I left Munich on what was supposed to be maybe a two-week trip at most. It ended up taking 81 bloody days or two months and three weeks to circle back to Renata.

I was actually surprised she took my call, let alone agree to pick me up at the bus station. I had a tough decision to make. Stay with Renata or go to Iyala. Tough choice because they were both wonderful women. I didn't know what to do.

That wasn't true. Iyala was the love of my life, my soul mate, so the answer was obvious. Still, I was tiring of having to make big decisions on the fly, so I decided to spend a week with Renata and then figure it out. Besides, after my many ordeals and close calls in the Middle East, I needed the rest. So, Renata and I ended up spending the week together.

We walked around the old city, often holding hands. We frequently went to our favorite pub. One night, we were there with her good friends, Fritz, and Ingrid. It was pretty crowded, so we ended up standing most of the time.

I noticed a guy sitting at a big table who kept staring at us. I asked Renata who the guy was; she said he was a friend she had recently been with since I wasn't around.

I then grabbed hold of her shoulders and pulled her to me. I gave her a long, deep kiss. When I let go, she laughed.

"You're so bad!"

"You bet your ass I am!"

I suppose my animal instincts came out, and, like an animal, I was marking my territory for the other animals nearby. The night went smoothly.

During the day, I fell into a normal routine. I still had the three chillums to ship to my Mom to give to my two brothers. The last one was for me. It was more expensive than I had thought. Oh, well. I wanted my brothers to have them since they were living in a religious cult right outside Los Angeles and had little in the way of material goods.

Renata's upstairs neighbor was a young guy who was our age and whose dad was Renata's landlord. He had an impressive record collection and told me I could borrow any album of his to listen to while I was there.

I picked a dozen of my favorite albums: Zeppelin, Stones, Doors, CSNY, and many others. I listened to them while Renata was at work. I also needed to catch up on my sleep before I hit the road again.

One night, the phone rang and woke us up. Renata answered, looked at me askew, and handed me the phone. It was my good friend Diz, calling long distance from Orange. Diz was known by a few names: Richard, his given name; Bimbo, which his father nicknamed him; and Diz, which I called him because he tended to drink a lot.

Diz and I raised a lot of hell together over the years. We spoke for half an hour, talking about my travels and what was going on in Orange. It was nice hearing from him.

A few nights later, I got another late-night call, this time from Michael in Germany. He was calling to see if I made it back. I explained what I had experienced on my trip back to Zurich, and he was fairly shocked. I told him I'd see him in Germany at a later date and went back to sleep.

It was now getting time to make my big decision. I couldn't just flip a coin, so I took a long walk in the forest while Renata was working. She was an elementary school teacher just outside of Zurich. I came to my decision that day, but the hard part was I had to tell Renata that night. I believed she knew I would be returning to Iyala; she knew me well enough during our short time together. She knew I would return to Israel because I had said I would, and she knew me to be a man of my word. And truth be told, it's what I really wanted.

That night, after dinner, we sat on the couch listening to some French jazz and talking. She broke the ice and asked me if I had made my decision that day on my walk? Damn, I thought, she knows me too well.

I told her I was returning to Israel. She nodded, saying she knew I had to. She was very understanding. Still, she cried some, so we held each other for a while.

I told her I'd be leaving in two days, so she took a couple of days off work. We hung out at the house, making love and listening to the great music I had borrowed.

There was one caveat. I needed to go to the U.S. Consulate in Zurich to get a new passport. I couldn't travel on this one any longer. I couldn't give them a forged passport. I had to lie and say I lost my passport somewhere in the city.

To get a new passport, I had to prove who I was, my identity. The only official proof I had for that was my international driver's license. Usually, they require a second form of identification, such as your birth certificate or your old passport. I didn't have either. Despite that, I had to try.

I walked to the consulate and got in line. I gave the pleasant, petite woman my international driver's license and told her my story. She said it might be difficult for me to get a new passport since they needed proof of citizenship. But she asked me to please wait, and she went through a door into an office.

A large bespectacled man in a fine suit emerged from the office. I thought he looked like the boss, which turned out to be true. I figured it was a good sign. He walked me to a door that led behind the counter to a back area and into his office. He offered me a chair and closed the door.

He looked at my license and said this wasn't sufficient proof of my citizenship. He asked me many questions, starting with did I lose my passport or was it stolen. I told him I didn't know. One moment, it was in my back pocket, and the next minute, it was gone.

He asked many more questions about where I lived and my history. This went on for 20-25 minutes. He looked at my driver's license again and then looked at me.

It was as if he had an epiphany. He nodded his head, chuckled, then walked over to his large closet. He returned with a four-inch stack of papers and dropped them on the desk in front of me.

He held up a picture of me from the stack and looked at me for verification. *"This is all about you, Tracy Miller. You have a very persistent mother."*

It seems my dear old mom had called anybody and everybody she could reach in Washington D. C., trying to get any help in finding me. The last correspondence she received from me was a postcard I had sent her before leaving Munich for Tehran. I wrote her saying I was going to Tehran and would be back in Zurich in a couple of weeks. Well, two weeks later, my trail had gone cold.

My mother knew me well. She also knew what was going on in Tehran. She assumed the worst, figured I was up to no good, and got on the phone. After all, she's a Mother, and mothers protect their children.

My mother, though, differs from others in one unique way. Within minutes of talking to her, she would know everything about your life. People feel so comfortable with her that they tell her everything.

Her detective work led her to a man in the State Department, or maybe someone in the CIA, because of what he was able to do for her. This man could trace my exact steps from Munich throughout Europe and farther east, even pinpointing the exact route I had taken to the Turkish and Iranian border.

He told her he had to stop his tracing of me at that point because of what I was up to and what was going on in Tehran at that time. He was afraid it would draw unwanted attention to me.

That's why I figured him for the CIA. He had to be to have had the contacts he had. I mean, only the CIA would have those kinds of contacts. Plus, he was able to tell her exact details about my trip that I only knew.

The man had this enormous stack of correspondence from Washington, D.C. all about me and my travels. The reason the Zurich consulate had it was because my Mother knew Zurich was one of my home bases where I was headed.

In a way, my Mom saved my ass. I could get a brand new passport the next day. I already had the passport pictures, so it was a quick turnaround, thanks to Mom and the CIA. I picked up my new passport, thanked the consulate employee, and was on my way.

Chapter 48

Back to my Girl

Renata and I got up early on the morning of my departure. I hitchhiked there. I had no other choice. After bribing what felt like the entire staff of Turkish guards, my money was running out.

Renata dropped me off at the highway entrance. She kissed me and then asked, *"Will I see you again?"* I said, *"Yes."* She drove off. I stuck my thumb out, and I was back on the road again, traveling solo, and it felt good.

I traveled the same route I came from, through Switzerland to Austria to Yugoslavia; then I'd head south through Turkey to Syria and on to Jordan. Once in Jordan, I'd enter Israel through the Allenby bridge. It was named after British General Edmund Allenby in 1918. Even though Israel and Jordon had no official relations back then, people could enter and exit through the bridge.

The last time I was in France, I went to the American Consulate in Nice to get a special passport. I had heard about it from a businessman I had met in Istanbul. I was borrowing the Hilton Hotel's shower (one of the nice hotels in Taxim Square) and stopped off in the bar to have a beer on my way out.

That's where I met the businessman, and he told me about the special passport. He did a lot of business in Israel and the neighboring Arab countries. He showed me his special passport and said it was a necessary item of travel. He used it all the time and strongly suggested I get one, though he confessed they were not given to just anyone.

WILD CHILD

He was right. I would need one because some Arab countries won't let you in the country if you have an Israeli stamp on your passport, and I had planned to travel more extensively throughout the Arab world.

I went to the consulate in Nice, France, and got in line and waited. When it was my turn, I walked up to the window and showed a tall, attractive woman with glasses my passport and explained what I needed.

She said there was no such passport, but I knew there was. We argued back and forth politely; then, an American businessman asked me if he could cut in since he had to catch a plane.

I said, of course, and stepped outside. He handed his passport to the lady and said it was his special Israeli passport; he then left to catch his flight. I smiled and politely informed her that I'd take that passport now. It took a few hours, but I walked out of the consulate with my new Israeli passport.

It was freezing outside, but I had a winter jacket made of sheepskin. It was also water-resistant so that it would repel the snow. I was thrilled to have it on this trip. That day was lucky since I got rides each time I was dropped off. I made it to Strasberg, spending the night at the youth hostel.

During the warm weather months, I would sleep on the side of the road, but not in the dead of winter if I didn't have to. I woke up early; I always liked to get an early start when I hitchhiked. I got a lot of long rides from truckers, but the first ride was from a businessman who picked me up and gave me a ride to the outskirts of town.

I walked down the road to a restaurant and stuck my thumb out. Almost immediately, a trucker pulled over. He was French and spoke very little English, so we just listened to music.

This was a great ride. He was driving to Belgrade, the capital of old Yugoslavia, which was over 500 miles. We stopped to use the bathroom and to eat. I bought him lunch that day, and he was grateful. We got to Belgrade the next morning. I love truckers; they book a lot of miles every day.

I was making great time on this trip, and I hoped it would continue. I was getting very excited about seeing Iyala again and holding her in my arms. However, it took a little longer to arrive at the Bulgarian border this time since most of the rides were from locals, so they were shorter rides.

It wasn't far to the border from Belgrade. I made it there that night, so I crashed outside on the Yugoslavian side of the border and cross in the morning.

It was cold, but I had a very good sleeping bag. Early the next morning, I crossed the border into Bulgaria and walked a short distance down the road. I wanted to stay close to the border crossing area because the truckers would be getting up to speed and were more inclined to stop and pick me up.

The Roaming Gods were definitely with me that morning. The first truck that pulled over was going all the way to Istanbul! Bulgaria wasn't a large country and Istanbul wasn't far from the Bulgarian and Turkish border, so we'd make it there that night, which was splendid news.

What a find the driver was. She was British and spoke the King's English. We would alternate friendly talks with the good tunes she liked. Her name was Bridget, and she was a middle-aged divorcee from Manchester, England, which was close to Blackburn, where my maternal grandfather was born and lived before he emigrated to America in 1900.

Bridget told me all about Blackburn and said one of her favorite pubs was there. We exchanged phone numbers. She told me to call her if I ever got to Blackburn, and she'd buy me a pint.

We made great time. Bridget was a bit of a crazy driver with that big truck of hers, so we arrived in the early evening, said our goodbyes, and I went straight to my flea trap hotel and crashed for the night.

Once I left Istanbul, I headed for Ankara. I got a ride through greater metropolitan Istanbul, meaning I was on the highway once again when another large truck pulled over.

WILD CHILD

He was German and spoke good English, so we talked all the way to Kayseri, just south of Ankara. He was heading east towards eastern Turkey to pick up a load. I was heading south from there towards Syria.

I was closing in on the Syrian border and got a quick ride just outside of the city. It took five rides to make it to the border late that afternoon. The last ride was going to Aleppo, just across the border.

Protests were going on here, too. More bloody protests! The Camp David Accords had just been signed at Camp David in America. It was a peace treaty between Egypt and Israel, something the Arab world wasn't too happy about; it was signed by the American President, Jimmy Carter, the Egyptian President, Anwar Sadat, and the Israeli Prime Minister, Menachem Begin.

I found a cheap hotel on the outskirts of town. It was an old majestic building, and you could tell it had been quite luxurious in its heyday, but that was a couple of centuries ago.

At the Syrian and Turkish border, the border guard wasn't really happy with me with all the current events. And since I was an American, he really had it in for me.

He told me, *"So you're going to Palestine to see your Israeli girlfriend on a kibbutz."* I told him, *"I've never been there, that I was headed to Egypt by boat through Jordan."* But he kept repeating it over and over, convinced I was lying. I just smiled because my passport was clean, and there was nothing he could do to me.

It took a couple of days to get to the Jordanian border because I was only getting local rides. If I had been driving, it would've taken less than a day.

My last ride dropped me off at the border on the Syrian side, so the driver didn't have to risk anything if I were doing something illegal. With my new passport, I crossed the border on foot with ease and stuck out my thumb.

I got a ride to Amaan with another trucker and ended up staying there for two days since I needed to get clearance to pass over the Allenby Bridge.

While I was waiting, I headed to Petra, the old Roman ruins that are these grand buildings literally built into a mountainside. Petra is south of Amaan, about halfway down the King's Highway to Aqaba.

I got there in a couple of rides and stayed for a day and a half. Then I decided to keep heading south to Aqaba, a beach city on the gulf of the Red Sea across the gulf from Elat in Israel. I figured it was about time this southern California beach boy could use some beach time and sun.

I stayed there for a week and a half, but it wasn't intentional. I had gotten sick with my second case of dysentery. Eating off of street carts will do that to you. I had neither the money nor the desire to see a doctor or admit myself to a hospital.

Since I had dysentery before, I decided to tough it out on the beach. The weather was nice, so I slept on the beach and met some great people, including a couple of Palestinians who told me their family had lived outside of Jerusalem in Ramallah before the 1948 Arab-Israel War of Independence.

I met a Kiwi, a New Zealand native. He had converted to Islam and was headed to Cairo to study the Koran. That is one of the beautiful things about traveling the world as I did; you meet so many interesting people all day long.

I woke up one day feeling better, still a bit sick, but better. I walked around town and found a small souk, a flea market on the street, and bought several old flannel shirts from an old man selling them cheaply. I was back on the road by mid-morning, heading back up the King's Highway.

I arrived in Amaan later that day, having gotten two long rides. The King's Highway was an interesting road. A lot of rich Saudis come to Jordan to play.

There was no alcohol or prostitution in Saudi Arabia, but there was in Jordan so that they would race up and down the King's Highway in their new Mercedes and Ferraris. If their cars broke down, they just left them on the side of the road.

I was at the money changer one morning, exchanging some of my German marks into Jordanian dinars. I had a small amount to change, but many Saudis exchanged their highly valued Saudi Arabian riyals into Jordanian dinars. The exchange rate was heavily favored on the side of the Saudis.

To watch the money exchangers, count money was a sight to behold. They would take a large stack of bills in one hand and flick them one by one with the other hand at great speed, counting the bills. They would make it through a large three-inch stack of bills in seconds and never make a mistake. They looked like one of the electronic money counting machines that are used by banks today. It was a work of art. I stood around watching them count for about an hour and then went on my way.

Chapter 49

Home

I arrived back in Amman and headed straight for the government building to pick up my clearance to cross the Allenby Bridge. I took a taxi to the bridge right away, crossed on the Jordanian side, and started walking to the Israeli side along the short bridge separating the two.

As I got closer to the Israeli side of the border, I could see the soldiers and started to get butterflies in my stomach. The soldiers looked like veterans doing their required annual two weeks of reserve service. Everyone in Israel, boys, and girls alike, does mandatory service in the Israeli army at eighteen years old. Boys do three years; girls do two.

Israeli soldiers are in the reserves until they reach forty-five years old. They are almost always called up when there is a conflict. Iyala's father was called up during the 1967, six-day war at thirty-seven years old and lost the use of both of his legs when the truck he was riding in hit a land mine at El Arish in the Sinai Desert.

The reservists don't always resemble the spit-and-polish types that most armies of the world do. When I saw them, it felt like home. Their shirts were untucked, unshaven, and one of them had an STP oil sticker on the butt of his American-made rifle. I considered Israel my second home, and that's what it felt like, a homecoming.

I crossed the bridge and headed straight for the bus station, using my new Israeli special passport. I thought I should call Iyala before I just showed up unannounced at the kibbutz.

WILD CHILD

I'd been gone for nine months but told her I'd be back in six. It's an old story on kibbutzim that a young kibbutznik falls in love with a foreign volunteer worker, and then the volunteer leaves saying they will be back, only never to return.

I called Shamir and was put through to the dining room, where everybody ate meals in the communal dining room. A young Danish volunteer girl answered the phone. It just so happened that she was a good friend of Iyala, and she chewed me out for being gone for so long.

I told her she was right but asked if Iyala was in the dining room? She told me she wasn't, so I asked her if she could get a message to her. She said, of course. I told her to tell Iyala that I was back in Israel and was getting on a bus from the West Bank heading to Shamir. I should be there this evening. She said she would go to tell her right away. I thanked her and told her I looked forward to meeting her.

I grabbed a shawarma from a cart and got on the bus for Kyrat Shemona near Shamir. The trip took longer than I thought. I had to change buses a few times and coupled with the wait times. It seemed forever before I would get there.

I arrived in Kyrat Shemona in the early evening and discovered I was too late for a bus to Shamir, so I called the kibbutz dining room, hoping someone I knew would be there. It was movie night in the dining room, so it was packed with people.

My old friend Asher answered the phone. He was in the Garin with Iyala; they were an army group of about a dozen soldiers stationed on the kibbutz for a couple of years of their military duty. I told him I was here in Kyrat Shemona but that the bus wasn't running.

He said he'd grab a van and get me. I imagined he told Iyala and a few friends in the dining room, which meant the whole kibbutz would know in minutes.

That was the way on the kibbutz. Anything that happened to someone in this small community in the morning was common knowledge by lunchtime.

I waited at the traffic circle for Asher to arrive. A couple of young Israelis came up to me, and we started talking. One of them was a young Air Force pilot named Benny that had just returned to Shamir from his military duty. The girl with him was a kibbutznik at the neighboring kibbutz, Kibbutz Amir.

Asher pulled up, got out, and ran over and hugged me. We spoke for a few minutes, and then he said, *"Let's get you back to Shamir. Someone is waiting for you."* That was good to hear. Though I knew in my gut that all would be fine between Iyala and me, my head wasn't as sure. But that's part of life.

We spoke on the way back to Shamir. Our two guests had known each other since they were kids because the two neighboring kibbutzim did many functions together.

The guy asked, "Why are you going to his kibbutz, Shamir?" He didn't seem too fond of me, and I wasn't sure why. I told him, "I had lived there before, that I was Iyala Mamony's boyfriend, and I had been gone for nine months with my traveling."

He responded, *"Oh, you're the one."* I smiled and said, *"Yes, and thank you; you just told me everything I needed to know."* His girlfriend laughed.

We dropped her off at the front gate of Amir, then headed to Shamir. As we headed up the hill and entered through the front guard gate, the realization hit me hard. I was home. We pulled up behind the dining room, where many of the kibbutz communal vehicles were parked.

We parked and got out of the van. I wished my new best friend well. I told Asher, *"I don't want to go to the dining room because I don't want to make a scene, and I also don't really want to talk to all my friends right away since it would take forever. All I want to do was see Iyala."*

He understood and said he'd tell Iyala I was here. I told him, *"I'd walk around to the front."* Soon as I was in front of the dining room, the door burst open, and there she was, my exotically beautiful Iyala, running full speed toward me.

I dropped my backpack and bag of new-old flannel shirts on the ground and ran toward her. We collided like two rocks and fell in a heap on the ground. We began kissing and hugging for about five minutes, right in front of the dining-room windows and most of the

WILD CHILD

kibbutz, effectively making the scene I didn't want to. At the same time, I didn't really mind.

We got up and walked to our new home. Iyala had moved to a nicer apartment on the kibbutz while I was gone. Once inside, we sat on the bed and talked and made love well into the morning.

Chapter 50

Back with my Girl

I woke up late the next morning. Iyala had already left for work. I got up and roamed around the kibbutz until lunchtime, saying hi to old friends and catching up with everyone.

I had lost a lot of weight on the road, especially with dysentery, and the kibbutz was the perfect place to get fattened up since there's always a lot of food served at each meal. I headed to the dining room for lunch. Many of my kibbutznik friends were there, and I ended up talking to everyone so much I barely had time to eat.

I got some food and made my way to Ehckeeam's table. I told him I wanted to come back and work for him in the fish ponds. He said, *"Of course, but didn't I want to take a few days off."* I said, *"No, I just came from a nine-month vacation."* Iyala entered the room, so I went over to sit with her and her Garin friends.

After lunch, I walked her back to work at the baby's house and then continued to roam around. I made my way to the volunteer ghetto and talked to some of the current volunteers for a couple of hours.

I saw Ehckeeam, Oded, and Vicko off-loading some fish into the storage tank on my way back up into the kibbutz. I walked over since I hadn't seen Vicko and Oded yet. We hugged each other and then stood around, talking for an hour. I told them a little about Tehran and invited them over after dinner to our apartment.

I picked up Iyala from work, and we walked home holding hands. We sat and talked about my travels and what she did while I was gone.

We both silently agreed that there was no need to talk about the other people we were with while I was gone. It was unnecessary. We were back together, and that's all that mattered.

Vicko and Oded came by after dinner, and we went down to the volunteer bar, drank some beer, and talked through the night. Iyala and I danced several dances together, and it just felt good to be back with my girl and hold her in my arms.

I had gained wisdom and knowledge about life and myself as I traveled around the planet. In my humble opinion, I had attended the college of the world.

Chapter 51

Back on the Kibbutz

Life got back to normal on Shamir quickly. I was working in the fish ponds again with Ehckeeam and Oded. Iyala was in the baby house, and all was wonderful. Vicko was now working on the cotton field and was very happy.

I thought I could spend my life here and was even strongly considering it. At one point, there was some talk about me taking over the fish ponds for Ehckeeam.

Cherney, a friend that worked in the mechanics' shop, mentioned it to me. Still, there was a big part of me that wanted to be an actor. I wanted to make that my life's work.

Iyala had finished her time in the army, and the only reason she was still in the kibbutz was because of me. Oded had also completed his army time and was getting ready to leave the kibbutz with Vicko. Iyala started spending more time at her home in Kfar Saba and weekends on the kibbutz.

We talked about going to Europe for a few months and then to the States for a while. Where we would end up living was something we didn't know yet.

We set plans in motion to hit the road together in a few months. In the meantime, with Iyala in town during the week and Oded and Vicko away, I spent a lot of time in the kibbutz by myself.

Instead of being a volunteer, I was now a guest on the kibbutz, which meant I was on track to becoming a kibbutznik. The order you followed was volunteer to guest to candidate to kibbutznik. You only reach the last stage when you are voted in by the members.

At one point, one of the older kibbutzniks I had worked with at the fish ponds discussed becoming one of the guards, protecting the kibbutz at night. I told him I'd be honored, so he started training me on how to break down and clean and shoot an Uzi machine gun. And for a short time, I was carrying an Uzi around with me. I usually left it at home or in the jeep; I felt odd carrying it around with me on the kibbutz.

Chapter 52

Making Money

The time was coming for Iyala and me to head for Europe, so I started winding down on the kibbutz. Iyala and I were spending more time in Tel Aviv and Kfar Saba.

As the time drew even closer, I left the kibbutz and took a job on a moshav down in the Negev Desert, working in the packing house. I needed to make some money to travel again, so I spent months working there, driving a forklift day and night, loading pallets of fruits and vegetables on trucks being taken to market.

I was working six days a week, twelve to fifteen hours a day. I came down with a virus and lost a lot of weight. By the time I left there, I was ultra-skinny.

The Negev is a scorching desert, and it was sandstorm season, so strong winds would blow sand everywhere. During these storms, sand would get in every crack of the house. To protect my living quarters from the sand, I'd put two sheets on my bed every morning before I went to work.

At night, when I came home, I would lift the top sheet, which was covered in sand; the bottom sheet would have a lot of sand on it, too. I would shake both of them off and brush off the bed before I could lie down to sleep.

I saw little Iyala during this period; she was working in Kfar Saba. She came down one weekend to visit, but other than that, we were both working.

WILD CHILD

One of her male cousins needed a job, so I got him one with one moshavnik picking fruit and vegetables. He only lasted two days and went home. I assumed he couldn't take the heat and hard work because he just left without saying a word. Not to brag, but I believe I earned Iyala's father's respect because I was a hard-working young man. And it didn't hurt that I sent him crates full of vegetables and fruits from the moshav.

Chapter 53

Hitting the Road... Again

The time was upon us. We were leaving in a few days, so I left my job on the moshav and headed to Iyala's house, where I would stay until we left. I was surprised her father would accept me staying in his house. I guess over time; I had grown on him.

The day finally arrived, and after saying our goodbyes to her family, we caught a bus to Haifa to catch the boat to Cyprus.

Once we boarded the ship, we found some deck space, and both of us settled into reading. Once we left port, the seas were calm, and the trip started wonderfully.

We arrived in Cyprus in short order since it's close to Israel. We got off the boat and found a restaurant Iyala loved for lunch. Cyprus is split into two halves, one for Greece and one for Turkey. They have had many wars over the years over territory.

We wandered around the island for a bit of sightseeing, just enjoying traveling, and she loved it. We stayed for a week and then got back on the boat for Santorini. We spent a few weeks hopping from island to island, taking our time. We also hit Ios, Mykonos, and Lesvos and just enjoyed ourselves.

We got back on the boat for a mellow ride to Athens. After about an hour out to sea, I saw Tim and Bruce's girlfriends walking on the deck. They spotted us and came over to talk. They told us that Bruce and Tim were down in the bar having a beer. They were headed for Athens, too. I folded up my book and turned to Iyala.

"It looks like our calm little voyage just ended." We went down to the bar, and Bruce and Tim were as surprised as we were to see them. Fate or coincidence brought us together on the same boat, headed for the same location.

We spent the rest of the trip drinking and having fun. When we exited the ship, we were pretty lit up and looking for more. We headed straight for a bar and continued to party. The only problem with that plan was, at this rate, I'd be broke long before we arrived in England to fly home.

We partied for a couple of days, then one morning, Bruce came to our room to tell us they were taking off. I thought it was probably a good thing.

After a few more days in Athens, we headed for Portugal via France and Spain. Iyala really wanted to see the Grand Cathedral of the Incarnation in Malaga down in the southern part of Spain.

So off we went from Milan, making many stops along the way. Traveling by train is a great way to see a lot of the countryside, and we took advantage of all the beautiful sites along the way.

While in Malaga, I lost our camera when I set it down and then forgot about it. When we went back, it was gone. We ended up in a huge fight and, in the heat of the moment, we split up, going our separate ways.

That lasted for about five minutes. I thought, what the hell am I doing, leaving her there to fend for herself, and this being her first time traveling and out of her country to boot.

I ran back and searched for Iyala for twenty very worrying minutes. I finally found her. She was sitting down in the middle of a walkway, crying and pulling everything out of her backpack. I ran up to her, sat down with her, and held her. I promised her I would never leave her again and that I would always protect her for the rest of our lives.

From Malaga, we took the train again to Lisbon, Portugal, which is another ancient and very beautiful European city that crashes into the sea from the cliffs; colorful homes also populate it. The food and weather were fantastic, and it is much less expensive than the rest of Europe, which we both liked.

We hopped on the train to northern Germany to visit my friend Michael from my Iranian adventure. Like the rest of our ongoing trip, we made numerous stops along the way.

When we arrived in Bremen, we found Michael with a girlfriend and a brand-new baby boy. He was still busking to earn his keep, and one night I went out with him to do some busking on the streets of Bremen. It was an interesting way to make money, to say the least.

We then headed into Denmark, a logical stop since we had many friends on the kibbutz who were Danish. We stayed with Iyala's friend, the one who answered the phone when I returned to Israel from traveling.

We then made our way to Amsterdam, a city I have always loved for its fun atmosphere. Once there, we went to the American Express office to get Iyala more traveler's checks. We told them she had lost hers. But we kept the old ones too. Not to cash them, but they wouldn't let her in England if she didn't have a good deal of money. Once in England, we destroyed the old checks.

We then made our way to the coast and boarded a ship to England, where we would fly back to the States. Once we arrived in England, we took our time, stopping along the way to sightsee.

We went to London for several days and then to the U.S. Embassy to finalize Iyala's American visa, which we had set up in Israel. The only way for her to get into the States was on a fiancé visa. That meant we would have to marry within three months.

They were supposed just to finalize it and stamp her passport. But often, Israel put pressure on countries to limit the number of Israeli's they let in their country, as they couldn't afford to lose citizens.

They wouldn't finalize her visa, so we were stuck in a hard place and needed to figure out what to do next. We decided we would use most of our remaining money to fly her back to Israel, and I would find a job to earn enough money to fly home later. It was a sad day when I put her on the plane for Tel Aviv. But I promised her I'd work it out from home, and she and I would be together soon.

Fortunately, our Israeli friend, Yosef from Iyala's Garin group, was selling cars to travelers underneath the Waterloo Bridge in London, so I stayed with him in his van.

Yosef told me they might be hiring at The National Theatre of Arts. I went and talked to the man who did all the hiring. He wasn't sure because most of the workers were from Yugoslavia, and he didn't want to upset the balance with me in the mix.

I told him I was a hard worker and friendly with almost anyone. I said I would only work until I earned enough money for a plane ticket back to the States. He hired me, and I ended up vacuuming floors for five weeks, five days a week.

When I was lucky, I worked on performance nights for extra money. One night, I was able to catch part of Richard Harris's performance in production. I only saw a little of it because it was off-limits to us.

During the day, I would go down to the bottom floor to eat lunch. All the young actors in the theatre's acting school would be there, eating and talking. Being around them only helped to cement my desire to become a professional actor.

Once I earned enough money, I purchased a ticket for my flight home. It had been just short of three years since I had been home, so I was looking forward to seeing my family and friends. A couple of days later, I was in the air, heading back to my homeland.

Chapter 54

Back in the States

When I arrived at LAX in Los Angeles, I had to go through customs, and the customs agent was another hard-ass. I could tell he didn't like the way I looked, but I didn't care. But I also couldn't blame him. I had long hair, a full beard, and hadn't showered or washed my clothes in a while.

There aren't any showers on the road or where I was staying, so I looked like a mess in retrospect. But after all the times I'd traveled through borders doing illegal things, I knew how to handle his type.

After all, this was my country, and I had nothing illegal on me; in fact, I hardly had anything in my backpack but my sleeping bag and dirty clothes. So I wasn't going to take any shit from him. I knew my rights, and since all my papers were correct, he couldn't keep me from entering my country.

When he gave me shit, I gave it right back. When he argued with me, I argued right back. This went on for a while, with me smiling from ear to ear. He wanted badly to find something, so he checked everything in my pack, but to no avail. He finally let me pass into my country, but only because he had no other choice.

When I saw my mother and kid brother, James, she asked me why I was arguing with the customs agent and said that I could.

My folks had invested in purchasing a gas station while I was gone, and things weren't going well. They had everything they owned tied up in it and were about to lose it all.

WILD CHILD

We stopped at the station to see my father and because my mom had to take care of some business. While I was there, I saw two young guys working there doing a lazy half-ass job. I thought I should fire them and train some new kids that wanted to work to earn their money. But it wasn't my business.

Little did I know that I'd be working there within a week because my folks were losing money and needed free labor. Within two weeks, we had all new employees that worked hard for their money. I worked seven days a week, ten to fifteen hours or more a day, which was nothing new to me. This went on for a year and a half until we got it to a point where we could sell the station for a profit for my folks.

I remember standing there one day, trying to figure out how the hell I had gone from traveling the planet and going to the college of the world to pumping gas in southern California.

All I could think of for an answer to my riddle was that life could make some radical turns that you're not expecting. But blood is blood, so you do what is necessary to survive. That my father and I never saw eye to eye didn't make things any easier to work there so damn much.

Chapter 55

Iyala Returns

It took three long months to work out Iyala's fiancé visa, but I finally did it. She picked it up in Tel Aviv, and her flight from there to Los Angeles was set.

The day arrived, and I anxiously awaited her flight at LAX. But there was one problem I didn't know about yet. She had a flight change at Heathrow Airport in London, and her flight was late arriving there. She had to run to catch her flight, but she ended up missing it. She stood at the end of the entry tunnel in tears, watching her flight pull away from her. She was able to get on the next flight and arrived in Los Angeles a few hours later than originally planned, so I just impatiently waited at the airport. When she walked down the exit ramp, we ran to each other and embraced. We held each other for a long time.

We stopped at the gas station so she could meet my folks and James. My Father was a real hard-ass, but he fell in love with Iyala immediately; most people do. She and James formed a very special bond, too, as did my Mother.

We ended up living at my parents' house for the first month, and that wasn't easy for either of us, especially Iyala. I worked so much; I was barely there. I had to do something. I ended up working out a deal with my folks to rent a one-bedroom apartment in town, and we were much happier.

Iyala got a job working at the local McDonald's and made many new friends. I worked like a dog, so she often ended up home alone. I'd take off as often as possible, and we eventually worked it out until we sold the station. We were finally settled in and content with each other in the States.

Three months later, we were married in a simple ceremony at someone's home. We told him to keep it simple since we didn't consider this an actual marriage but the last step of the visa process. And that when it was time, we'd have a real wedding or two, meaning one in the States and one in Israel.

Chapter 56

The Road's Lessons

In my travels, I learned a good deal about myself, life, people, and the world that would serve me in many ways in life.

I learned that I could deal with almost anything that came my way in life with more grace and confidence, based on how I dealt with life before this trip. I had built up a good deal of confidence in myself through all the trials and tribulations I went through on the road.

And I had a better understanding of people and the world. I understood much more about human nature in many different situations that always come up in life.

They were good life skills that would serve me for many years to come, especially as an actor. I had a stronger understanding of what makes people tick and many difficult situations to pull from as an actor. It made me a calmer man for someone who had never been a cool head and let his feelings and emotions control him. I pull from these experiences daily in my life today.

The End

About the Author

Tracy Miller is the first-time author of "Wild Child," a memoir of a young man's wanderlust, roaming the planet via thumb and backpack back in the 70s. His story chronicles the mischief he encountered along the way, from being arrested in Munich as a suspected terrorist to being stuck in Tehran during the '79 Iranian student revolution. From his time on a kibbutz to being robbed at knife point, to working his way around the world, embracing life at its lowest and finest, this is the story of a man who followed an extraordinary path out of drug addiction and petty crimes and, in the process, found the better part of himself, as he studied life at the college of the world and became a better man for it.

Born in Southern California, Tracy developed a yearning for travel as a military brat. He is also an award-winning actor of 38 years and continues to work in the industry he loves, having won 6 best actor awards at film festivals around the country. He is the father of three children and a grandfather to one. He is also a pretty good pool player, falling somewhere between Jackie Gleason and Paul Newman. He currently lives in Southern California.

You can keep abreast of Tracy's career as an author and "Wild Child's" progress at www.tracymillerauthor.com.

TRACY MILLER

Made in the USA
Las Vegas, NV
21 April 2024

88976916R00118